GW01607164

Bozzimacoo: *Origins & Meanings of Oaths & Swear Words*

Bozzimacoo: *Origins & Meanings of Oaths & Swear Words*

by Mary Marshall

M & J Hobbs in association with Michael Joseph

First published in Great Britain by
M. & J. Hobbs
25 Bridge Street
Walton-on-Thames
in association with
Michael Joseph Ltd
52 Bedford Square
London, W.C.1
1975

ISBN 0 7181 1380 2

Set and printed in Great Britain by
Tonbridge Printers Ltd
Peach Hall Works, Tonbridge, Kent
in Plantin ten on eleven point
on paper supplied by P. F. Bingham Ltd
and bound by James Burn
at Esher, Surrey

CONTENTS

ORIGINS

Origins

To my husband, whose idea it was in the first place

Introduction

What do you say if a large heavy object falls unexpectedly on your toe? *Oh bother,* perhaps? Of course to some extent what you say will depend upon your age and sex, but I suspect that if you've got as far as reading this introduction your exclamation might be a little stronger than *Bother*.

The same mishap to your toe in the 14th century might have stung you to a *Gog's Malt*, in the 16th century to a *Sdeath* or *Zooterkins*, during the Restoration to an *Adzookers* or *Zauns*, in the 18th century to a *Niggers Noggers* or *Cats Nouns*. In Victorian times, alas, you couldn't have said much, perhaps a *Dash it, Ding bust it,* or *Blankity Blank.* And today? Certainly there aren't many words you couldn't say if you wanted to. Regrettably the fashion seems to be for less and less variety and more and more four-letter words.

As this is a history of oaths and swearwords it's important at the outset to define what are the oaths and swearwords we're talking about. Originally to swear or take an oath meant that you made a serious statement or promise, calling upon some gods, saints, supernatural powers or something you held sacred to confirm the truth of what you said or the binding nature of your promise. Today the definition of swearing is much wider.

Technically you are swearing (though it's unlikely anyone will object much) if, however lightly, you refer in exclamations or emphatic phrases to the devil – *What the dickens*, supernatural powers – *By Jove*, saints – *By George*, religious characters – *Holy Moses*, famous personalities in fact or fiction – *Crippen*, even to natural phenomena – *Holy Smoke*.

You are also swearing (and here people might start objecting) if your exclamations contain references to God or Christ, to the afterlife, especially if uncomfortable (*Heavens* is all right but *Hell* and *Damnation* less so); and if in any connection whatsoever you use certain words, particularly *Bloody* and various four-letter words, held to be vulgar and obscene. This last is the type of swearing that offends people most.

You may choose to disguise your swearing by substitutions and euphemisms, with a *Golly* for God, *Cripes* for Christ, *William III* for turd and so on, but you're still swearing in intent, though in the most delicate way.

Why men swear is a psychological question beyond the range of this introduction. In passing, it's intriguing to note that American Indians, Japanese, Malayans and most Polynesians don't swear at all. The rest of us seem always to have needed a vent for our pent-up emotions, rather as a boiler needs a flue. For this purpose explosive and sibilant consonants suit us best. (The sets of cards in my alphabetical index of swearwords are thickest under *b, g, d, p, c, s* and *sh.*)

The words of our oaths have differed from one century to the next, but there's not much doubt that man has been swearing in the wide modern sense of the word ever since he could speak. Most of the four-letter words are very old etymologically. Profanity seems equally long established: certainly the Almighty found it necessary to include a strongly-worded reminder about it in the Third Commandment.

Unfortunately for the researcher on the subject, oaths and swearwords belong to spoken far more than literary language. The amount of early material is therefore somewhat limited. In the absence of tape recordings of the Ancient Greeks or Britons swopping oaths and imprecations we have to rely on the often meagre literary sources.

The Ancient Greeks

νὴ τούς θέους

The Greeks were well endowed with deities to swear by. Their most common oaths were *By Apollo, By Hermes, By Demeter,* and sometimes by all the gods at once (*νὴ τούς θέους*). Aristophanes' prize-winning comedy THE FROGS (405 B.C.) contains the equivalents of just as many *Plague take you*'s, *Damn You*'s and *Bless me*'s as you'd expect to find in a full-blooded Elizabethan play, though not the vulgarisms or obscenities. Greek women too were apparently as outspoken as their menfolk. According to Phrynichus the Grammarian, their favourite oath was *νὴ τόν Δία, By Zeus* (the father of the gods). Their children were allowed to swear *By Hercules* but not in the house. They could do it in the streets if they liked.

Not all the Greeks took their religion seriously, and some of their oaths were decidedly flippant. Socrates, for example, *By the dog, the goose, the plane tree,* and – of all prosaic things – *the cabbage.* (For the strange explanation of this oath, see section on MEANINGS).

The Romans

'Quaevis numina'

The Romans swore along much the same lines. They had adopted most of the Greek gods, only pausing in the takeover to change the names, from Hermes to Mercury, Demeter to Ceres, and so on. Popular Roman oaths were *Ecastor* and *Edepol* ('*By Castor*' and '*By Pollux*', the Heavenly Twins), and *Mihercule* or *Hercle* ('*By Hercules*', the classical Samson). The Romans appear to have taken oaths while holding a special sacred stone, probably a meteorite, called the *Jupiter Lapis* or stone of Jupiter, and these words too may have become an oath. The Latin poet Virgil swore poetically enough by the earth, sea and stars; Ovid, a more cynical contemporary, swore by *Quaevis numina* – by whatever gods you please. The Roman emperor Caligula, murdered in A.D. 41, ordained that Romans should swear only by his, the emperor's head. He had the strange idea that his health depended on the amount of swearing being done.

On the whole the Romans, like the Greeks, seem to have avoided obscene words and oaths. Cicero the famous orator recommended public speakers to avoid the word *cunnus* (from which our four-letter word is derived) though poets such as Martialis and Catullus hadn't the same delicacy and did use it.

The Anglo-Saxons

We know that at this time formal oaths were taken very seriously. The Anglo-Saxon CHRONICLE of 877 describes how Guthrum the Viking invader swore a treaty of peace with Alfred, taking an oath on a certain holy ring. Then Guthrum broke his oath, continuing to ravage the English countryside and making a surprise attack on Exeter. But trouble was in store for him. A frightful tempest overwhelmed the Danish sea army and a hundred and twenty ships were sunk. Many must have seen this as a divine retribution for oath breaking.

The same could be said of Harold Godwinson's defeat at Hastings in 1066, if the Bayeux Tapestry is to be believed. Shipwrecked and captured in Normandy, Harold had been tricked by William into swearing a feudal oath (he promised to become William's liege man for life), possibly over the bones of St Edmund. Whatever version of the story is to be believed, Harold seems to have been in a Heads You Win, Tails I Lose position. If he refused to take the oath he might never have seen England again, let alone the English crown. If he swore it, he had either to break it or accept a sizeable demotion from the Throne of England to the Earldom of Wessex.

For the other sort of oaths in this early period, the blasphemies and profanities, there is negligible literary evidence for the southern half of Britain. There are some old statutes from the reigns of the Scottish kings Donald VI and Kenneth II which show that draconian measures were felt necessary to curb the evil habit of swearing: the penalty for the foul mouthed was cutting out the tongue.

The Normans and Plantagenets

With William the Conqueror firmly seated on the English throne, and his nobles and their fighting men suitably rewarded with English estates, French became the language of the ruling classes, of the lawcourts, schools and universities. Not until the end of the 14th century did English begin to take over again.

The Normans were a tough soldiering nation, only two or three generations removed from Viking pirates. Neither the Norman kings nor their Plantagenet descendants were mealy-mouthed. William's favourite oath is said to have been *By the splendour of God*, his son Rufus's *By the Holy Face of Lucca* (a northern Italian town with a miraculous crucifix). A century later Richard Coeur de Lion favoured *God's Legs*, and his brother John Lackland *God's Teeth*.

Another popular Norman oath, less regal perhaps, was *Datheit*, 'grief or misfortune to'. When an English writer used it in 1338 he turned it against the French. '*A Breton, dayet his nose*', he wrote. In more modern English: 'A Breton, damn his nose . . .'.

Vernacular oaths of the early Norman period are few and far between.* This is because most literature written in English before about 1250 consisted of religious works, such as the lives of saints and collections of sermons. These were intended for the instruction of the lower classes and are hardly a likely source for swearwords. There are plenty of pious emphatics such as *For Godes love* and *For Godes grace* scattered through the pages, but the phrases are used utterly reverently.

However there must have been some irreverence about. Various

*I have come across *By Driytin* (from the Anglo-Saxon word for god) and *O dews* (from the Latin *deus*) used in much the same way as we might exclaim *Oh God* today.

moralists were deploring the evil and widespread practice of swearing. In 1340, for example, a Kentish monk called Dan Michel devoted several dreary pages in his AYENBITE (The Remorse of Conscience) to the abuses of the different sorts of swearing. 'Some men,' he said 'are so evil taught that they can say nothing without swearing... (using such oaths as) *by my father's soul, by the fire that burns, by my head,* or other such like'.

Whether or not the poor English serfs were muttering anything stronger under their breath as they slaved away for their Norman landlords, at the top of the feudal pyramid the oaths were elegant French ones, such as *parfay, pardieu,* and *depardieu.*

This was the age of chivalry, a code of conduct which was strictly observed by knights and ladies at the English and French courts from the 11th to the 13th centuries. One convention of the code was the formal oath often taken by bands of knights before any important expedition. An early 14th century poem LES VOEUX DU PAON describes how a great banquet would be held and a roasted peacock placed before the lady of greatest rank or beauty. Then the carver, and after him all the knights present, would pledge themselves in the name of '*God, our ladies and the peacock*'. Edward I took the Vows of the Swan in 1306 when he knighted his son before invading Scotland.

Chivalrous knights were pure in speech. (That was the theory at least, though one wonders about the heat of battle.) But it was quite permissible for them to use asseverations such as *By God, God wot, By Mary, Christ reward you,* provided they were reverent in tone. In the 13th century poem SIR GAWAIN AND THE GREEN KNIGHT the conversation is full of such phrases, the more significant since Gawain was traditionally the most courteous of all knights.

A Chaucerian cross-section

'By Goddes Love'

At the end of the 13th century comes one of the best early records of contemporary speech. This is Chaucer's CANTERBURY TALES, a mine of information about swearing habits of his time. The band of pilgrims journeying from London to Canterbury is a real cross-section of society, a market-researcher's delight.

From what one might today call the AB social group there is for example a sober and serious knight, his son a young squire who is a chivalry fanatic, and a refined, rather affected prioress. From the middle class there's a doctor, a franklin, and a bawdy housewife from Bath. Still lower down the scale, there's a drunken miller, a pardoner and summoner constantly squabbling with each other, a greasy cook and a sailor.

Chaucer varies his language most skilfully to suit the individual characters and so provides a splendid insight into the vernacular of the day. Bear in mind too that he was writing for a predominantly aristocratic audience. So the crudities and four-letter words he uses (*queynte* and *arse* both appear) must have been acceptable at court.

It's worthwhile examining the oaths used by some of the different pilgrims.

The Knight is most restrained, using only a few conventional *God wot*'s, *By my fay*'s, and *By Goddes love*'s. In his courtly tale of two knights who are rivals for the same lady he also includes a *By mighty Mars,* indicating he has had the right sort of classical education. His son the Squire favours the occasional French oath such as *Par Charitee*. Chaucer may have been taking the mickey out of those solemn oaths on the swan and the peacock when he has Sir Topas, the hero of the Squire's Tale, swearing

'By ale and bread
How that giant shall be dead'.

A rung lower in the social ladder we have the gaptoothed uninhibited Wife of Bath. Frank as she is about her enjoyment of sex some vestigial modesty makes her use the Latin *quoniam* as a substitute for *quointe*. (She claims her husbands told her she had '*the best quoniam mighte be*'.) But her oaths are noticeably more frequent and less restrained than her social superiors'. *Lord Christ,* she exclaims, *Good lief, By Peter, By God and by St Joce,* as well as many a trivial *Pardee, By my troth* and *By my fay*.

The Shipman, as befits a seasoned traveller, favours oaths incorporating the names of various continental characters such as St Martin of Tours, St Ive of Brittany and St Denys of France. The Miller, drunk most of the time and author of the coarsest tale of all, swears freely and variously *By Cristes sweete tree, By St Note* (better known nowadays as St Neot), *By St Frydeswide* and *By armes, blood and bones*.

If the Miller is the most ribald of the pilgrims, the Host, Henry Bailley, is certainly the most profane. He has a fund of different oaths, some of them, such as *By corpus bones,* the weirdest mixture of ill-digested Latin and English. To give a small selection only, he swears *By God's two arms, By St Paul's bell, By God's bones, By St Ronyan, By the Trinity* and *By nails and blood*.

It's very likely Henry Bailley did exist. There are records of a Harry Bailly who was an 'ostyler' or innkeeper in Southwark. If Chaucer's description is to be believed he was as free with obscene swearwords as with oaths. At one point he loses his temper completely with the Pardoner. This wily character has neatly wound up his tale with an appeal to his listeners to buy his pardons and kiss his relics – at a price, of course. 'Not on your life' says Henry Bailley:

'But, by the cross that St Eleyne found,
I wish I had thy coillons in my hand*
Instead of relics or the seintuarie.†
Let's cut them off, I will thee help them carry;
They shall be shrined in a hog's turd.'

At one point the Pardoner piously deplores the current abuse of swearing by every conceivable portion of the Saviour's body, but he

*Testicles.
†Holy objects.

doesn't follow his own advice, and gives as good an oath as the next man.

It is left to the country parson to put a genuine case against swearing. '*For Christ's sake,*' he pleads, 'Swear not so sinfully, for you dismember Christ when you swear by his soul, his bones and his body. For certainly it seems that you think the cursed jews did not dismember the precious person of Christ enough and you want to do still more of it.' (This idea that Christ's body is torn by each oath on His person was a recurrent theme in anti-swearing tracts and sermons for several centuries.)

The parson also rebukes Henry Bailley personally for his swearing, after one set of *Goddes bones* too many. The innkeeper promptly accuses him of being a Lollard. (The Lollards were followers of the reforming preacher Wyclif, indignant at the corruptions of the contemporary church. One of their favourite issues was the abuse of swearing.)

It's a pity there was no soldier on Chaucer's pilgrimage. Had there been, Chaucer's vocabulary might have been even riper. Certainly there would have been a good few *Goddam*'s, the name by which English soldiers were known up and down Europe because of their hearty swearing. A few years later than Chaucer, Joan of Arc promised her men Goddams for supper before she led her victorious army to Orleans. Apparently Joan did attempt to clean up the language of her own barrack room: she curbed the vocabulary of La Hire, her friend and comrade at arms. He was only allowed to swear in her presence if it was by his marshal's baton.

Some early Yorkshire oaths

'Kiss the devil's toute'

In the early 15th century there are miracle plays such as the WAKEFIELD SHEPHERDS PLAY, written very much with a working class audience in mind. It's full of earthy oaths and swear words such as *Come kiss myne arse, What the devil of hell, Kiss the devil's toute* and *The devil in thy maw.* Mak, a Yorkshire shepherd who has been trying to put on refined airs and graces, as if he came from the sophisticated South, is told firmly by his fellow shepherds:

'Now take out that Southern tooth,
And set it in a turd.'

The oaths in the play are so frequently and casually interpolated in the speeches that they would hardly have had much force. There are mangled Latins tags like *Benste and Dominus,* workaday oaths like *By my hood* and *By the rood,* and the traditional invocations to the *Virgin, St Thomas of Kent* and so on.

Swearing by the Saints

St Thomas of Kent, whose shrine Chaucer's pilgrims were on their way to visit, was one of many medieval saints and martyrs. Most of their names have little significance for us today, but our ancestors swore by them and to them with a will. Today who has heard of *St Joce, St Frydeswide, St Cutberd, St Quenet* or *St Loy*? They all featured in popular 15th century oaths. Many saints were of course associated with particular occupations, qualities or places. If you were a blacksmith you might well have sworn *By St Loy* (*St Eligius*). If you were a cripple you could try *St Giles*. If your shoe pinched an appeal to *St Crispin,* patron saint of cobblers, might have done some good.

Few saints remain in the modern swearer's vocabulary. Even *By St George* (our patron saint) has dwindled to *By George*. We owe the disappearance of all these saints and martyrs to Henry VIII and the Protestant Reformation. After Henry's U.D.I., as far as the English Church was concerned 'The Romish doctrine concerning Purgatory, Pardons, Worshipping and Adoration, as well as of Images as of Reliques, and also Invocation of Saints, is a fond thing vainly invented'.*

A modern eavesdropper on a 15th century conversation would certainly have had his problems. He would miss the relevance of

*Article 22 of Cranmer's Prayer Book of 1552.

many a saintly oath. He would also find it hard to unscramble some of the stock oaths of the day. *By cock's precious podstick,* for example, sounds hilarious and is barely identifiable as the original devout *By God's precious body. Bigog, Gog's malison, Bumtroth* and *Bomfay* sound like nonsense words from Carroll's 'Jabberwocky' rather than everyday oaths.

The Tudors

In 1534 the Act of Supremacy was passed, culmination of the Reformation in England, and for Henry VIII a temporary solution to some pressing marital and fiscal problems. Reformation there may have been in the Church, but not, one gathers, in the swearing habits of either the working man or the Court.

Poems, tracts and disapproving sermons continued to pour out denouncing the 'horrible oaths' men were using. Even children, said Sir Thomas Elyot in his BOKE NAMED THE GOVERNOUR, 'play with the armes and bones of Christe as they were cherry stones'. Ten years after the Act of Supremacy a pamphlet entitled SUPPLYCACIOUN TO KYNGE HENRY THE EYGHT appealed personally to the King to end the nationwide abuse of swearing. Henry was hardly the man to apply to. True to the long-established kingly habit he was no mean swearer himself. At least three of his children followed his example.

Sir John Perrot, one of Henry's illegitimate sons, is credited – almost certainly wrongly – with inventing the oath *Christ's wounds.* Perrot was a favourite of his half-brother Edward VI and is said to have regaled the boy for hours with tales of his mis-spent youth. Maybe his language influenced the young prince a little. Certainly Edward started his reign with a flurry of oaths.

The anecdote is recorded in the LITERARY REMAINS OF EDWARD VI. It tells how the rather priggish little boy, succeeding his father at the age of nine, let fly in public with a few *God's blood*'s and *Christ's passion*'s. He said a friend had told him that kings always swore. The friend was promptly whipped, with Edward made to look on and feel guilty. (No one could administer corporal punishment to the royal person.) Edward meanwhile perhaps wondered why it was wrong for a young king to swear and not for the powerful nobles round him.

When Elizabeth came to the throne in 1559 she was certainly too old to be reprimanded about strong language and proceeded to swear like a man till the end of her reign. Two of her favourite oaths are said to have been *God's death* and *God's teeth*. Her court ladies preferred the milder *Zooterkins*. (See MEANINGS.)

The Elizabethans

'Gerry gan the ruffian clye thee'

At the opposite end of the social spectrum, among the criminal classes, swearing was equally hearty but cruder. Thomas Harman's CAVEAT FOR COMMON CURSETORS, (a warning for common vagabonds) published in 1567, explains and translates some thieves' cant – 'lewd lousy language' he calls it – for the benefit of honest citizens. According to Harman a popular cant oath was *Gerry gan the ruffian clye thee,* which he translates as '*A torde in thy mouthe, the devylle take thee*'.

Elizabethan plays provide us with plenty of examples of swearing, both U and non-U. In declamatory tragic scnes the high-born protagonists lard their speeches with *Zound*'s, *Pox*'s, *S'blood*'s and *Slid*'s galore. Lower down the social scale, in the comic scenes of Shakespeare's and Jonson's plays, for example, the vocabulary is less elevated. Rather franker oaths and insults are exchanged such as *I fart at thee, Hang it, Thou whoreson knave* and *A turd i' your teeth.*

No wonder the Puritans were scandalised by the theatre. Indeed the strong language in contemporary plays was one of the main arguments in their persistent demand for closing down all London's theatres.

According to Philip Stubbes, in his ANATOMIE OF ABUSES of 1583, the plays of the time 'maintain bawdry, insinuate foolery and renew remembrance of heathen idolatry'. At the theatre, he continued, 'you will learn to swear, tear and blaspheme both heaven and earth'. Stubbes was equally critical of the 'abundance of alehouses, taverns and inns' and the behaviour of the drunks or 'Malt-worms', as he scathingly called them: 'How they stut and stammer, stagger and reel to and fro like madmen . . . and which is most horrible, some fall to swearing, cursing and banning, interlacing their speeches with curious terms of blasphemy, to the great dishonour of God, and offence of the godly ears present'.

Oaths in conversation were taken so much for granted that they could be used by card sharpers for a simple cheating system. Says one professional cheat in A MANIFEST DETECTION OF DICEPLAY, 'Ye know this outrageous swearing that some use in play . . . We have but lightly these: "*of honesty*", "*of truth*", "*by salt*", "*Martin*", which when we use them affirmatively, we mean always directly the contrary. As for example, if haply I say you when the dice cometh to your hands "*Of honesty cast at all*", my meaning is that ye shall cast at the board or else very little. If when a thing is offered in gage, I swear "*By Saint Martin I think it fine gold*" then mean I the contrary, it is but copper.'

One last comment from the period, on the Elizabethan sprig of fashion his strange attire and lusty speech, from Thomas Middleton:

'That which struck us most in admiration, upon those fantastical boots stood such huge and wide tops, which so swallowed up his thighs, that had he sworn as other gallants did, this common oath "*Would I might sink as I stand!*" all his body might very well have sunk down and be damned in his boots.'

'A turd i' your teeth'

The Stuarts

'A pox on all and sundry'

In 1603 Elizabeth was succeeded by James of Scotland, a noted blasphemer. On a foreign magnifico commenting on the king's fluency an English courtier replied that it was all a sign of His Majesty's gentleness. The foreigner was somewhat bemused and the courtier had to explain that James was perfectly aware of his powers to punish but preferred to leave the offender to Providence.

A strapping *God's wounds* was his usual oath, but he was not above wishing a pox on all and sundry when in a bad temper. He also had a taste for lavatory humour, judging from some of the anti-masques or comic interludes in the court masques Ben Jonson wrote specially for him. Happily he was somewhat stricter as a father, according to the historian Clarendon. His eldest son Henry had to put money into a swearing box every time he swore. Clearly a case of Do what I say, not Do what I do. The method seemed to work though. When Charles I succeeded his father (Prince Henry died young) he 'could never endure any light or profane word' says Clarendon.

Meanwhile the Puritans continued to urge the closure of the theatres, and tracts and sermons streamed out about the evil habit of swearing. In 1611 one by the Dean of St Paul's was printed, entitled A SWORD AGAINST SWEARERS.

1623—Swearing becomes illegal

Pressure was mounting. At last in 1623 an Act of Parliament was passed which made it a legal offence to swear. For every oath or curse there would be a fine of one shilling, to be used for the poor. If the offender couldn't pay up he would be put in the stocks, unless under twelve years old, in which case he would be whipped by the constable, parent or master. The law must have been tricky to enforce, but there are records in contemporary quarter sessions of offenders paying up for oaths as mild as *Upon my life* and *By my troth*.*

In Cromwell's army even the soldiers had to pay their shillings. Sometimes the penalty was worse. One quartermaster had 'his tongue bored with a redhot iron, his sword broken over his head and himself ignominiously dismissed the service'.*

Under the 1623 Act the poor were the beneficiaries. Others perceived that such a scheme could net attractive revenues for state or monarch. In Elizabeth's reign her Secretary Burghley had been approached by a man named Rodenburg who assured him that it ought to bring in twenty million crowns, but nothing was done. Charles I, ever in need of money, actually set up a Department of State to do the job. Under a man named Lesley it was to repay him with two and sixpence in every pound raised. Lesley appointed deputies for every parish and they were to keep a further two and sixpence. The plan seems to have failed, probably to the accompaniment of further bad language, though it was raised again from

*Ashley Montagu. THE ANATOMY OF SWEARING.

time to time. (Who knows, if only some foolproof legislation could have been devised to catch enough offenders and bring them to justice we might well be paying less income tax today.)

Life in the eleven years of the Commonwealth must have been a little too Spartan. The Puritans had had their way at last and theatres were closed down in 1642. But the pendulum swung to the other extreme when Charles II returned to rule in 1660.

The Restoration

'ods Niggers Noggers'

Charles' thoroughly dissolute court provided the bulk of the patrons for the theatre. The plays of the period therefore are a tolerably accurate reflection of the tastes, habits and language of the court. Never before had such licence been allowed on stage. Of the subject matter one successful playwright, George Farquhar, observed in one of his prefaces 'A play without a beau, cully,* cuckold or coquette is as poor an entertainment to some palates as their Sunday dinner would be without beef and pudding.'

These beaux and coquettes swore with a will, peppering their conversations with the latest modish oaths. *Piss, A pox on it, S'death and fumes, Daggers, Stap me vitals,* the men would exclaim, and the ladies *Oh fie, Pish, Good-lack-a-day*. (Charles is said to have taught the ladies of the Court to 'swear like parrots'.) Strange distorted forms were fashionable, such as *Udsbud, Save, Cods my lifekins, Adad, Oons, Ods Niggers Noggers.*

There was also a vogue for French catch phrases and oaths which some members of the 'ton' overdid a bit. In BURY FAIR, the dramatist Shadwell mocks the affected French manners of Lady Fantast and her daughter, with their *mondieu*'s, *morbleu*'s, *ventre bleu*'s and *teste bleu*'s. The two of them are bamboozled and quite transported

*Woman's dupe.

with delight by a French hairdresser pretending to be a Comte.

Bloody also seems to have been rather an 'in' word at the time, used freely by both sexes, but not yet as forceful as it later became. After a horrible description of children being bayoneted, Lady Fantast exclaims '*This is very bloody*'. Sir Humphrey Noddy calls the French barber a '*bloody rogue*'. And Shadwell himself dedicated another play, THE SULLEN LOVERS, to Prince William because he hoped this would give him some protection from the '*bloody hands of the critics*'.

It was very important for a young gentleman up from the country not to appear the country bumpkin. Listen to young Squire Mockmode in Farquhar's play of 1698, LOVE IN A BOTTLE. He is getting advice on speech and pronunciation from the affected fop Rigadoon. Mockmode feels he must learn to dance, play upon the flute and swear the most modish oaths.

Mockmode: Pray, which are the most fashionable Oaths in Town? *Zoons*. I take it is a very becoming one.

Rigadoon: *Zoons* is only used by the disbanded Officers and Bullies: but *Zauns* is the Beaux pronunciation.

Mockmode: (having taken some snuff) *Zauns,* I must sneeze. (Sneezes) *Bless me*.

Rigadoon: Oh fie, Mr Mockmode! What a rustical expression that is. – *Bless me!* – you should upon all occasions cry Dem me. You wou'd be as nauseous to the Ladies, as one of the old Patriarks, if you used that obsolete expression.

The licentiousness and profanity of court and stage was passing all bounds. There was an atmosphere of cynical materialism too, as one visitor noticed. A colonist, lately returned from the New World, he approached an officer of State to ask him for help in saving colonists' souls. 'Souls', he was answered, '*Damn their souls!* Make tobacco!'

On a wave of mounting criticism of court and stage a Society for the Reformation of Manners was founded in 1700. But it was troubled by a diversity of aims, as such societies often are, and was also criticised on other familiar grounds: there were complaints that the members, while displaying a tender regard for the morals of other people, were distinguished by a marked absence of virtue in their own personal lives.

The moral standards and language of the theatre were passionately attacked by Jeremy Collier in his pamphlet A SHORT VIEW OF THE IMMORALITY AND PROFANENESS OF THE ENGLISH STAGE, published in the same year as Farquhar's play. Collier deplored the continual swearing in stage dialogue. He was also thoroughly steamed up about the unsympathetic characterisation of clergymen on the stage – not surprisingly as he was one himself.

17th & 18th century oaths and obscenities

'The Cull has Rum Rigging, let's Ding him, and mill him and Pike.'

There are some other interesting sources for oaths and swearwords of this period, though not strictly 'literary' ones. A certain B. E. Gent adopted Thomas Harman's idea of collecting and explaining contemporary thieves' cant. In 1690 or thereabouts he published a short dictionary of the 'terms ancient and modern of the Canting Crew'. 'Useful', the subtitles continue, 'to all sorts of people (especially foreigners) to secure their money and preserve their lives; besides very diverting and entertaining, being wholly new.' Most of the cant terms would indeed have been unintelligible to the majority. B.E. gives as one of his examples: '*The cull has Rum Rigging, let's Ding him, and mill him and Pike*'. This he translates as 'the man has very good clothes, let us knock him down, rob him and scour off'.

B.E. lists some of the slangy oaths and obscenities of the canting crew, *Kiss my blindcheeks,* and *Rake hell and shim the devil,* for example. Rather disparagingly he also includes two 'silly curses in use among the Beaux': *Split my windpipe,* and *Stap my vitals.*

Another rich source is the writings of Ned Ward, landlord of the

King's Head Tavern near Chancery Lane at the turn of the century, author of racy pamphlets such as A VADE MECUM FOR MALT-WORMS, and the second invaluable publican in this introduction. He has been called 'the most colloquial of English writers' which is one way of putting it: if you want to know some of the seamier early 18th century expressions for whores, homosexuals, breasts and bottoms this is the place to look.

Ned Ward was as liberal with oaths as some men with commas, and a strange assortment they were at this period. The latest manglings of the word *God* were *Ud, Ad, Cud* and *Cat.* The popular oaths, among the tavern fraternity anyway, were *Adsheartiwounds, Cats nouns, Udslidikins, Uds niggers noggers, I'fackins, Zooks* and *Cuds bobs.*

Cautionary tales from Bunyan

Not that the man in the street – or the pub – got away uncriticised with his oaths and obscenities any more than the upper class fops. There were many thunderings from Sunday pulpits, notably from Dissenters like Bunyan – when he was out of prison, that is. In or out of prison he churned out books and tracts with fantastic speed. In 1680 he produced a moral tale called THE LIFE AND DEATH OF MR BADMAN. The story is told in a dialogue between Mr Wiseman and Mr Attentive. In Mr Wiseman's opinion his countrymen swore so heartily because they thought it 'gentlemanlike to be a damme-blade, saying *God damn me, God perish me*'.

Bunyan offers some Struwelpeter-type cautionary tales as deterrents. He quotes the 'dreadful judgement of God about one N.P. at Wimbledon in Surrey; who after a horrible fit of swearing at and cursing of some persons that did not please him, suddenly fell sick and in little time died raving, cursing and swearing.'

Then there was the hair-raising story of Dorothy Mately, from Ashover in the County of Derby. Poor Dorothy. On the 23rd of March 1660 she was washing ore upon the top of a steep hill and was rash enough to wish that the ground might swallow her up. It proceeded to do so. She was last seen disappearing into the ground while still 'twirling round and round in her tub'.

The anti-swearing pamphlets and tracts continued into the 18th century. Steele in the TATLER and Addison in the SPECTATOR both wrote satirical essays on the 'foolish habitual custom of Swearing'. Those who took the problem more seriously were worried how to catch offenders in flagrante, so to speak. One suggestion was a system of paid informers in every village, hardly good for community relations.

Dr Johnson and Dean Swift

Morals, on stage at least, seemed to be improving. Licentious plots were disappearing. Language was cleaner, though oaths were still very fashionable in aristocratic dialogue. It's at this period that the so-called dirty words started going underground. When Dr Samuel Johnson published his mammoth dictionary in 1755 the story goes that he was approached and congratulated by an 18th century Mrs Mary Whitehouse for not including any nasty words. He responded with typical acidity, asking her how she knew he hadn't – had she been looking for them?

Dean Swift, on the other hand, though professing to believe in 'proper words in proper places' did use four-letter words in his writing. Indeed he seemed to want to shock readers by the frank use of foul language, maybe because of some mental hang-up. However when he wrote in a much-quoted letter to his great friend and ex-pupil Stella, that 'it was bloody hot walking today', the word was still only an intensive like the modern 'terribly' or 'frightfully'.

Modern readers can get a good idea of the type of inanities exchanged over 18th century tea cups from Swift's satire POLITE CONVERSATION. Not that the vapid and banal remarks are very different from what you might hear at a modern cocktail party. However Swift, with tongue in cheek as usual, apologises for one striking omission in the book: there are no oaths.

He explains that he left them out because so many extra words would have doubled the size and production costs of the book. There was also the problem of keeping up to date: by the time the book was published the oaths would be out of fashion.

While on the subject of oaths, Swift had one significant recommendation to make to male readers. 'I most heartily recommend' he writes, 'that they would please a little to study variety. For it is the Opinion of our most refined Swearers, that the same Oath or Curse cannot, consistent with true politeness, be repeated about nine Times in the same Company, by the same Person, and at one sitting.' Perhaps this barb was directed at one particularly inarticulate social dolt whom Swift had suffered from.

Earlier than POLITE CONVERSATION Swift had dashed off another broadside, THE SWEARER'S BANK, a send-up of inveterate swearers and foolish investors. The pamphlet was published in 1720, year of the South Sea Bubble trouble, when there was an incredible mania for speculation. (At the time investors were sinking their savings in the most ludicrous-sounding enterprises. One company was promoting Puckles Machine Gun, which, it was claimed, would use square bullets on the Turks and round ones on the Christians.) Swift's mocking proposal for an Irish bank based on the revenues from fining swearers one shilling an oath, with exemptions guaranteed for the armed services and patients under medical care, seems hardly more far-fetched than some of the other schemes being floated to con the gullible public.

Swift reckoned the revenues from swearing would be huge and would 'vie with the South Sea Company'. For to take an example nearer home, in London alone 'there are computed to be one hundred pretty fellows that swear fifty oaths a head daily; some of them would think it hard to be stinted: this very branch would produce a vast sum yearly'.

Profane Oaths Act in operation

With his shilling an oath fine Swift was referring to the old Profane Oaths Act of 1623, several times ratified in the 17th century. It was still not working too well, so a tougher version was enacted in 1745. Rather a class-conscious version, this one, discriminating between labourers, sailors and soldiers, who would only be fined 1s. for swearing, and more respectable folk below the rank of 'gentlemen' who would have to pay 5s. The proceeds were to be given to the poor of the parish. If an offender could not pay up, it was off to the house of correction with him.

In 1751 an unfortunate woman who was indicted for a single oath was fined a shilling, and as she couldn't pay it she was packed off to the Bridewell prison for a week. One wonders how the system worked for a burst of swearing on an empty purse. Did the tradesman indicted for 390 oaths in the same year pay up, or go to jail for nearly eight years?

Any justice of the peace or constable who failed to act upon information received was also liable to be fined. The Act was to be read one Sunday every quarter in every parish church and public chapel. Two parsons who failed to do this were fined, the richer £15 and the poorer £5. The case sounds intriguing. The sons of the poor parson, bearing a grudge against the wealthy one, had reported him for dereliction of duty – without first checking that their father had done his stuff. Incidentally the Act was not repealed until 1967.

It's hard to say what effect the Act had. One anonymous gentleman disagreed with it strongly enough to publish A SHORT AND MODEST VINDICATION OF THE COMMON PRACTICE OF CURSING AND SWEARING OCCASIONED BY THE NEW ACT OF PARLIAMENT AGAINST THE SAID PRACTICE.

But in upper circles profanity seems to have been on the decrease. In Sheridan's stylish comedy THE RIVALS, first produced in 1775, Bob Acres says categorically that *damn*'s 'have had their day' and proceeds to try to sell the idea of the 'oath referential or sentimental'. To swear with propriety,' he goes on 'the oath should be an echo to the sense'. Arriving after a breathless journey, he exclaims: '*Odds whipps and wheels*, I've travelled like a comet'. After a musical evening he comments '*Odds minims and crotchets*, how she did chirrup at Mrs Piano's concert'.

The idea, not surprisingly, did not catch on. But the point is that Acres felt that 'propriety' in conversation was important. The novels of the period reflect the same tendency. In Goldsmith's VICAR OF WAKEFIELD, first published in 1766, throughout a series of family disasters the strongest oaths are *a Murrain take such trumpery, A bots on you* and *Confusion seize him*.

The Navy, the Army and Francis Grose

In Smollett's last novel HUMPHREY CLINKER (1771), the characters swear noticeably less than in his earlier books. Admittedly HUMPHREY CLINKER lacks the swashbuckling naval and military types of the earlier RODERICK RANDOM (1748) and PEREGRINE PICKLE (1751) which gave Smollett such enormous scope to exploit his own experiences as a surgeon aboard a British man-o'-war and sometime inmate of the Fleet prison for libel. Smollett certainly comes up with some splendid nautical oaths in the early books, positively reeking of the lower decks, such as *Smite my timbers, Splice my old shoes* and *Ads buntlines*.

Indeed the navy's reputation for foul language was such that one Mathew Towgood moved house to a sea port so he could study the bad language of sailors in their natural haunts. The result of his research was a pamphlet UPON THE PROFANE AND ABSURD USE OF THE MONOSYLLABLE DAMN, published in 1746. For the oaths of the back streets at this period we can consult Captain Francis Grose's CLASSICAL DICTIONARY OF THE VULGAR TONGUE, first published in 1785. This is underworld cant again, with some interesting observations on various oaths and swear words thrown in for good measure.

In Grose the four-letter words are printed with asterisks or dashes, though the definitions are fairly unrestrained and some of the comments and examples are not for delicate stomachs. (There are crude proverbial catch phrases such as *He would lend his a-se and sh-te through his ribs, To piss by the pot,* and a most scatological explanation of the nickname *sh-t-sack* for a Nonconformist preacher.)

Judging from this dictionary the four-letter words were not yet used as expletives, though *Ax my arse,* a constant since the 14th century at least, was still going strong.

It seems Grose had little time for the Irish. He quoted several Irish oaths with disparaging comments. *Arrah now,* he defines as 'An unmeaning expletive, frequently used by the Vulgar Irish'; *Holy Father* as 'a butcher's boy of St Patrick's Market, or other Irish blackguard; among whom the exclamation or oath *By the Holy Father* ... is common'. *Dear Joys* is another nickname for Irish men, 'from their frequently making use of that expression'.

Grose includes several other interesting oaths. *Salmon,* he explains, is the beggar's solemn oath; this must have been a steady cant tradition as the word was first recorded in the 16th century. *Gadso,* another common oath, is not an innocent corruption of *God save us,* says Grose, but 'an exclamation said to be derived from the Italian word *cazzo* (penis)'. *Dead Chelsea by God,* another oath, was the exclamation of a soldier wounded at Fontenoy, delighted that he would be sure to be invalided home to the Chelsea Military Hospital. (For more oaths from Grose see in the MEANINGS under *Damn* and *Nation.*)

Grose's Dictionary spanned the end of the 18th and beginning of the 19th centuries. The first edition came out in 1785, the fifth in 1823, which sounds as if there was a pretty steady demand for the product. Thereafter no further edition was published until Partridge's annotated reprint of the third edition in 1931. Even at this late date Partridge felt it necessary to have the book privately subscribed and limited to such a small number 'that not even the most censorious could take exception'.

The 19th Century and the Victorians

'Gorblimey'

The hundred odd years separating the last two editions were an age of euphemisms. In polite Victorian society even the legs of pianos were hardly to be mentioned. Hideously embarrassing words such as men's trousers were known variously as '*indescribables*', '*ineffables*', and '*unutterables*' (and as '*sit-upons*' among the slightly less genteel). Not surprisingly a careless oath or loose word in the drawing room spelt social suicide – in mixed middle or upper class company anyway.

The Armed Services still had a bad name for swearing. The Duke of Cambridge, for instance, earned a frown from Queen Victoria for letting slip some language which did not amuse her. The Duke of Wellington too seems to have waged a minor campaign against swearing at officer level. When inspecting the Grenadier Guards one day he asked their colonel to check an officer who was swearing at his men. The colonel replied that the officer in question had lately come from a Line regiment, as if this explained everything. Perhaps it did, for all Wellington had to say, so the story goes, was 'Oh! Ah!'.

The lower classes, meanwhile, both military and civilian, continued in the same gutsy strain as before. Pierce Egan's LIFE IN LONDON of 1821 quotes the sort of language you might have heard at the time from the lips of undesirable females such as Dirty Suke and Squinting Nan, who call each other '*dirty bunters*'. Suke swears by her '*precious sparklers*', and puts her case with many a *Blow me tight* and *So help me Bob*.

There are more glimpses of the same lingo in Mayhew's study of LONDON LABOUR AND THE LONDON POOR, and in samples collected by philologists such as 'Ducange Anglicus' and the German Heinrich Baumann, whose LONDONISMEN of 1887 includes the words *bloody* and *bugger*.

It was almost as if there were two social languages as in the old days of the Norman Conquest. One was for the working classes, alleviating a desperate poverty with gin and ripe language, the other for the rest of society. The prosperous new middle-classes were particularly busy aping the manners of the aristocracy, determined at all costs to be seen – and heard – to be proper.

In the 'other' London, in the gin palaces of the period, you would have heard a stream of Cockney oaths, such as *I'll be gormed, gordelpus, gorblimey, strewth, I wish my bloody eyes may drop out.*

According to Julius Sharman in A CURSORY HISTORY OF SWEARING, 1884 this word *bloody* was the hardest worked word of all in such circles: 'From the low-lying quarters of the towns the word buzzes in your ear with the confusion of a Babel. In the cramped narrow streets you are deafened by its whirr and din, as it rises from the throats of the chaffering multitude.'

But the word could never be heard or even hinted at in polite society. *Bloody* is an example of Victorian hypocrisy. The word is not blasphemous (see MEANINGS) but it was considered to be extremely vulgar, working-class and therefore outrageous. Even the common euphemism *ruddy* was barely acceptable. In 1887 Sullivan named the latest Gilbert and Sullivan opera RUDDYGORE with a pun obvious to all. Middle-class theatre goers were – or pretended to be – appalled. The theatre management persuaded Sullivan to accept a change in the spelling to RUDDIGORE. Further than this he would not budge.

Victorian gentlemen were permitted to swear if they restrained themselves to the sort of euphemisms quoted by Chas. T. Tallent-Bateman, writing for the Manchester Literary Club in 1886, expressions such as *By jabers, By ginger, By jeremy, By jerry, By gilliver, By giggery, By jilly, By Gemini*. There were a host of extraordinarily silly oath-substitutes, which must have sounded ridiculous from the lips of grown men, such as *Godfrey, Jumping jehosophat, Blankity Blank* and *Therewith.*

Others were more ingenious and effective, often using puns and assonance to good result, as in *Cheese and crust, by heckelum, Helen Maria.*

Many of the best euphemisms of this period came from the United States. Perhaps this was because there was a particular need to let off verbal steam: pioneering was tough going. But being godfearing folk the new Americans created oaths which couldn't offend, such as *I'll be dadburned, Grease us twice, I'll be dingswoggled.*

Victorian literature reflects for the most part the bowdlerised language of the middle-classes. Upper and middle-class heroes and heroines didn't swear. In typical late Victorian novels such as JOHN HALIFAX GENTLEMAN and MRS HALIBURTON'S TROUBLES in which virtue goes through the most harrowing trials but emerges unscathed, the long-suffering heroes are permitted a *By George* and *On my soul* here and there, but nothing stronger.

Such emasculated prose seems unreal. Fortunately it's not all we have to go on. Dickens, with his accurate ear for dialogue, presents something nearer to reality. In NICHOLAS NICKLEBY, for example, the two 'languages' can be seen side by side. The virtuous Nicklebys (mother, daughter and son) can under provocation let slip *For God's sake, Fie upon you, For pity's sake, Upon my word* and *Bless me.* The oaths of Ralph Nickleby and Sir Mulberry Hawk brand them at once as the villains of the piece. *Damme,* they say, *Egad, Devil take me.*

At a more homely social level there is Miss Squeers of Dotheboys Hall exclaiming *Lawk* (see MEANINGS) and the landlord *Lord love you* and *Ecod.* Of all the characters the Yorkshire coachman, John Browdie, has the widest vocabulary of oaths. He's full of *Stars and garters, Dang my bootuns, I'm darned, Odds bobs, Ecod, Ding me.* None of these oaths could possibly offend a Victorian reader, but at least this sounds like genuine vernacular speech.

'Not Bloody Likely'

The strong middle-class taboos on real swearing were lifting at the turn of the century. Judging from Bernard Shaw's picture of contemporary society in PYGMALION, *bloody* was considered permissible for gentlemen: Professor Higgins, says his housekeeper Mrs Pearce, uses it three or four times in as many minutes when in a bad temper, and she begs him not to use it in front of Eliza. Mrs Eynsford Hill, representing the older generation, confides to Mrs Higgins that she will never be able to use 'that word', implicitly condoning its use by her daughter, the silly snobbish Clara.

At the first performance of Pygmalion in 1914 the whole audience gasped as Eliza uttered the shocking words '*Not bloody likely*'. One wonders now what all the fuss was about: it was not the first time the word had been heard on stage; the audience knew perfectly well what Mrs Patrick Campbell as Eliza was going to say. Were they pretending to be shocked, or was it, as I prefer to think, an early blow for Women's Lib? The reaction was surely because a respectable female was using the awful word in public.

The word was sufficiently respectable during World War I to appear in the caption to a Punch cartoon. Indeed during the war the English soldier (and even more his Australian comrades) was as internationally notorious for his *bloody*'s as his earlier counterpart, fighting against Joan of Arc, had been for his *Goddam*'s. In the crop of war novels published in the twenties *bloody* appeared in full, and became acceptable again in print. On stage too it was permissible, after Shaw had made the running, though the number of *bloody*'s per performance was for a long time limited.

Four-letter words in the 20th century

'F***'

The line was still drawn in print at the worst crudities. Certain four-letter words never appeared in a printed text. Even in dictionaries bold enough to include them they were asterisked. Until 1960 it was held to be a legal offence, except in reprints of earthy old classics like Chaucer, to print either *cunt* or *fuck*. (There had in fact been one or two unfortunate accidents in the past. Ashley Montagu, in his ANATOMY OF SWEARING, quotes the mystifying appearance of the word *fucking* on two separate occasions in the same year [1882]. And this in the respectable columns of THE TIMES. The first time the word was incorporated in the report of a speech made by the Attorney General; the second in a publisher's advertisement for a thoroughly establishment publication about EVERYDAY LIFE IN OUR PUBLIC SCHOOLS. Readers and printers of the paper expressed their consternation. Sabotage was suspected, but the culprit or gremlin was never found.)

Godfearing parents were still bringing up their children to avoid naughty words. One correspondent described to me her father's way round the problem of setting a good example in such matters: 'My father's favourite expletive – in front of the children anyway – was GODfrey DANiel Simpson's BLOOD manure works and BLAST furnaces.' (Kate Sawle Daly of Camberley.)

But permissiveness was growing. With World War II came widespread tolerance for some pretty coarse service slang terms, such as *Up shit creek without a paddle, Shit, piss and corruption, Cunt cap* (a service forage cap) and *Drop a bollock.* After the war James Jones' FROM HERE TO ETERNITY was one of the many war novels published. This particular one was a gritty account of life in the U.S. army in the Philippines. It was notable for a liberal sprinkling of *fuck*'s and *shit*'s, printed in full – according to one count nearly 200 instances. (Rumour has it that when the original MS was submitted to the publishers it contained nearer 500.) The publishers completely expunged from the text two further four-letter words, probably feeling that they had gone far enough.

In FROM HERE TO ETERNITY the four-letter words were used either as straight expletives, or with the verbal suffix '-ing' as pejorative epithets. In another notorious novel, LADY CHATTERLEY'S LOVER, D. H. Lawrence used *fuck* and *cunt* in their literal sexual sense. This was all part of his crusade 'to labour always to make the sex relation valid and precious'. At first he only succeeded in achieving the opposite: because of the four-letter words and several explicit sexual descriptions the book gained an ill-deserved pornographic reputation.

The book was first published, in a bowdlerised version, in 1928. The complete text was published in England by Penguin in 1960 and became the subject of a law suit. It was something of a cause célèbre and many literary celebrities testified in its favour. The verdict was for the publishers. Ever since, the two coarsest four-letter words have been permissible in print.

It's one thing to read such words. To hear them pronounced or pronounce them yourself is a further big step in permissiveness. The other media – television, radio and cinema – lagged behind in this respect.

Gradually the breakthroughs have come, such as Kenneth Tynan's studiedly casual use of the word *fuck* on B.B.C. T.V. in 1965. The same word, in its literal sense, was even heard on B.B.C. WOMAN'S HOUR in 1972, though there was a torrent of disapproval from listeners. Lately live T.V. reports, such as documentaries from Ulster, have contained four-letter words which programme directors have no longer felt obliged to cut. In this respect American television is still stricter than British.

In the cinema the censor has eased up considerably. Films such as LAST TANGO IN PARIS would never have passed the British Board of Film Censors a dozen years ago (on the grounds of language as well as the notorious butter scene). The language in such films still offends a lot of people, but the argument for permitting it is of course 'they don't have to go and hear it'.

Strong language, according to the Secretary of the British Board of Film Censors, is still one of the factors taken into account in licensing films. One of the Censors' major problems is the universality of English itself. Words which might be acceptable in a British film on circuit in England might not be tolerated in the States and vice versa.

The growing American negro film industry allows far stronger and cruder language than most British or white American film goers are prepared for. Australian English films, such as THE ADVENTURES OF BARRY MCKENZIE – sort of Commonwealth Tom Jones – are far freer with oaths and obscenities than British films but if you can stomach the crudities the gusto of the language, especially the oaths and swear words, is a tonic.

This brings me to the end of the historical part of the book, and practically into the MEANINGS section, where individual oaths and swearwords are treated in more Ruddigory detail.

This section contains a great many euphemistic oaths and substitutes for offensive swearwords. Often the formation of these euphemisms deserves a closer look. Many, especially in the U.S., have been created by deliberate spoonerisms, such as *Smoly Hokes* and *Mist Alcrity*. Others such as *Cheese on crackers got all muddy* and *Helen Maria,* grew from assonance and puns. Intialising is another wellworn disguise for strong language masquerading in polite society. Often the initials are so well-established that the original meaning has been forgotten. This is the case with the U.S. *S.O.L.*, *T.S.* and *S.N.A.F.U.* (See under *B.F.* for the transliteration.)

Another fairly transparent disguise is rhyme, particularly among Cockneys with their tradition of rhyming slang. Often the rhyming element is left out, as in expressions such as *Like the good friar* (with Tuck understood) and the commonly used, derogatory noun *Berk,* short for *Berkeley Hunt* and a lot more insulting than many speakers realise.

The MEANINGS section is alphabetical as this seemed the simplest both for readers and author. It would have been possible and might have been fun to arrange all the swearwords in groups according to professions, nationalities and even age-groups.

To start with the youngest, there are schoolboy and schoolgirl oaths, such as *Crumbs, Disguddy blusting, Hells bells and buckets of blood*. These oaths have a smell of mothballs about them: nowadays the average school kid's swearing vocabulary is hardly distinguishable from his Dad's. There are transient cult oaths like Batman and Robin's *Holy Basket Balls* and *Jibooms and bobsleighs;* trade oaths like the 17th century butchers' *By horn and hoofe,* and the Irish butcher boys' *Holy Father;* cant oaths like the beggars' *By the salmon,* and the thieves' *Newgate seize me;* nautical and military oaths like *Caulk my deadlights* and *Damn my eyes and limbs.*

Then there are the literary oaths specially coined for a particular context like Sheridan's 'oaths referential', or oaths which the author uses to give a period or national flavour, like Sir Walter Scott's weird French oaths in QUENTIN DURWARD. (Where on earth did he get hold of the extraordinary oath that never was, *Biftek de mouton?*)

Fitting into no particular category but impossible to leave out are the oaths in the 17th century translation of Rabelais' PANTAGRUEL. I have included some of these in the MEANINGS section because though they can hardly be taken as typical of the ordinary speech of the time, the panache, originality and fluency of the oaths – pages and pages of them with hardly any duplication – must be almost unrivalled in the English tongue.

Many swearwords are associated with particular nationalities. As early as 1628 a writer was categorising the swearing habits of different nations. 'The German', he said, 'swears in his highest puff of passion on a hundred thousand sacraments; the Scots bid the Devil take their soul, but the Welshman swears by his sweat'. Today too, if you couldn't pin a man down by his accent, you might well be able to do so by his oaths. *Tare an' ouns, Bejabers* and *Holy Mother of God* are unmistakably Irish. *Goddamit, Dad burn it, By crackity,* equally surely American.

In the 20th century many colonial oaths have breezed into England. Not always the most elegant of oaths, to be sure, and tending often to the graphically earthy. However, expressions from Australia such as *Strike me up a blue gum, Starve the lizards* and *Stone the mopokes,* have an outlandish charm for the insular Englishman. Australians are particularly fond of interpolating *bloody* into any convenient word that happens to be around – *Goodbloodymorning* and *Himabloodylayas,* for example. You could call it a transplanted epithet.

Bloody is a great divide among the English-speaking nations. It never caught on in any pejorative sense in the United States, but in Australia and New Zealand it is still working as indefatigably as in the Mother Country.

We desperately need new oaths, like the recent Australian imports. The present state of the English swearer's vocabulary is parlous. Oaths almost more than any other 'in' words lose force with over-use. As Swift wrote in 1720,

'Men change their oaths
As often as they change their clothes.'

Some oaths of course do last longer than others, particularly the strongest obscenities and profanities. To take an early historical example, *Christ's wounds,* one of the most enduring of oaths, started round about the 14th century as a most serious and terrible oath. Gradually it was corrupted and emasculated to the ubiquitous *Oons, Zoons,* etc., of the 17th and 18th centuries. Probably the original charisma around the oath made it more durable than most. But in the end it too passed out of currency.

Nowadays the fashionable trend is for the language of the building site. Few people have thought where this development will lead. In fact there simply won't be any swear words left after the four-letter words have lost their impact. To extend Swift's simile, there are no clothes left in the swearer's wardrobe for him to change into.

There are two possibilities. There could be a clamp-down and clean-up of the language. There are straws pointing in this direction, such as the proposed Cinematograph Bill which would make it an offence to reproduce by any means of sound reproduction 'indecent sounds whether or not consisting of words' at public performances. But at the moment despite all the efforts of Mrs Mary Whitehouse or the Festival of Light, there seems small likelihood of a mood of Puritanism sweeping the country.

The other possibility is to make use of our magnificent oathy heritage. I have compiled this collection of oaths and swearwords, by no means exhaustive, to suggest just how much is available. Readers at a loss for an oath or two are invited to browse through it. Whether you like your oaths to be Cockney rhyming, breezy colonial, coarse Chaucerian or ingeniously euphemistic, you should find something to suit your tastes and invigorate your vocabulary.

Meanings

Aballiboozobanganovribo
A whopping ten-syllable nonsense oath used by the Victorian poet Southey, instead of other naughtier words.

Adod, Adad
17th century corruptions of *Afore God*. These forms were carried to the New World by English colonists. *Idad* and *Edad* were heard as late as the 1920s in some Western States of the U.S.

Ads Bobbers, Ads Zookers, Ads Wauntlikins
These extraordinary sounding oaths are 17th century corruptions of *God's body, God's hooks* (nails) and *God's wounds*. – Likins is a common diminutive.

Ads Buntlines
A naval version of the above. A buntline is a rope attached to the sails of a ship.

Almighty Dollar, by the
A euphemistic oath from the U.S. Probably the origin was a remark made by Washington Irving in 1836. The 'Almighty Dollar' he said, was 'worshipped throughout the land'.

Almighty Fishooks (Gosh)
Another U.S. euphemism: *Gosh* is for 'God', *Fishooks* for embellishment.

Arrah
According to Captain Francis Grose, compiler of a fascinating DICTIONARY OF THE VULGAR TONGUE in 1785, this word was 'an unmeaning expletive frequently used by the Vulgar Irish'. (Grose seemed to have it in for the Irish: see also *Holy Father*.)

Arri
If you ever needed to express annoyance or surprise in Hottentot, this apparently was the word to use.

Arse, Kiss my, etc.
Printable till the mid-18th century, but always earthy. *Kiss my arse* or *the devil's arse* were early English insults familiar to all classes. Dean Swift the cleric was still using the cut down version *My arse*

in the early 18th century. Then the word went underground, surfacing occasionally in vulgarly vivid compounds and catch phrases such as the 18th and 19th century *My arse on a bandbox,* or 'Thanks for nothing' (Because a bandbox would be so inadequate for the job), and the later *Arse-cooler,* or bustle. In dialect the word was always more decent, used in good expressive compounds such as *Arsey-varsey,* or topsy-turvey, *Slither-arse,* slippery material, and the proverbial *Pot calling the kettle black arse.* (N.B. For standard English this proverb had to be cleaned up.)

Since the 1930s *Arse* has been back in print, together with many modern elaborations on the old insults. Interestingly, the word is less shocking in the U.S. than in Britain. Perhaps because U.S. pronunciation and spelling allows the speaker or writer the benefit of the doubt. (In U.S. English *Ass* can be bottom or donkey.)

Bad Cess to you, Bad Scran to you

The best of bad luck to you. 19th century Anglo-Irish oaths. *Cess* is probably an abbreviation of *Success. Scran* comes from an old word meaning to scrounge food.

Balderdash

Originally 'frothy nonsense'. Nowadays often used as a euphemism for *Balls* (q.v.) especially in rolling compounds such as *Balderdash, poppycock and piffle.* Smollett's grumpy Matthew Bramble complained that London wine was '*vile, unpalatable, balderdashed with spirit and the juice of sloes*'.

Ballocks, Bollocks

An expletive of extreme annoyance. Of ancient Anglo-Saxon stock, from the Old English *Bealluc,* a bull's testicles. The modern use as a verb meaning to reprimand is probably from a pun on *Bawl* and *Balls.* Long before *Ballocky Bill the Sailor* was heard of, *Ballocks* and *Cods* were 17th century nicknames for the parson and his curate.

Balls

Nonsense, with obvious semantics. The word and its euphemisms have been a standby for swearers for centuries, from Rabelais' '*May my bauble be turned into a nutcracker*', to the modern *Balls, bees, and buggery,* or more delicately, *Balls, picnics and parties.*
(Euphemisms: *Whirligigs, Tallyways, Cobblers* [q.v.], *Knackers, Nags, Pebbles, Apples, Nerts* [q.v.].)

Bally

Victorian euphemism for *Bloody* (q.v. with three possible etymologies: (i) The pronunciation of *Bl——y,* Victorian printers' favourite way out of the problem. (ii) The abbreviation of *Ballyhoo,* short for Ballyhooly, a proverbially noisy town in County Cork. (U.S. *Hooey* has the same origin.) (iii) An adaptation of a Victorian Music Hall catch phrase 'Tell them the Ballyhooly truth' which was probably a euphemism, by reversing the syllables, for 'the whole bloody truth'.

Banchoot, Beteechoot
Quoted by George Orwell as unforgivable insults in Hindustani. Literally: you sleep with your sister (*Ban*) or daughter (*Betee*).

Barnum, Great, Ye Shades of P.T.
American jocular pseudo-oaths, after Phineas Taylor Barnum 1810–91, the great showman and ringmaster.

Bastard
Originally not a pejorative, but the officially recognised title for the son of a man of rank and his concubine. In Australia and the U.S. the word has always been tolerant and affectionate rather than rude.

Bath, Go to
Victorian Southerners' euphemism for *Go to hell.*

Bedad, Begar, Begob, Begok, Begox, Begum, Begummers
Old local yokel corruptions of *By God.*

Beggar, I'll be Beggared
Well-established euphemisms for *Bugger,* etc.

Begorra
Corruption of *By God,* a traditionally Irish oath.

Bejabers, Bejaises
Corruptions of *By Jesus,* from the Irish pronunciation 'Jay-sus'.

Belakin
See *Lady.*

Berk (You)
More insulting than many users realise. *Berk* is the abbreviation of *Berkshire* or *Berkeley Hunt,* which in its turn is rhyming slang.

Bethmons
By the man. See *Bithmon.*

B.F.
Bloody Fool. Now has an old-fashioned ring. Initialising is a well-established way round offensive phrases in polite company. Often the initials can be translated properly or improperly, as circumstances warrant. (The well known *S.N.A.F.U.*, for example, can be rendered quite harmlessly as 'Situation Normal All Fouled Up'; *T.S.* as 'Tough Sledding'; *S.O.L.* as 'Short Of Luck'.)

Bitch
An early 19th century slang dictionary rated this 'the most offensive of all insults to an English woman'. Has lost much of its force since then. A common euphemism is 'five-letter woman', paralleling 'four-letter man'.

Bitching
Favourite Australian rude intensive. The usage goes back at least to Chaucer, who wrote about '*Bicced bones*' (dice).

Bite, Bite me, Frost Bite me, Dog Bite my ear
Victorian lower-class oaths.

Bithmass, Bithmaskins
See *Mass*.

Bithmon, Bethmons
19th century dialect forms, especially Lancashire and Cheshire, of *By the man,* itself a euphemistic oath.

Blank it, Blankity Blank
Euphemisms, mainly U.S., from the 'blanks' in *B——t* and *D——n.*

Blarm me
Corruption of *Blimey* (q.v.).

Blast
Now mild but originally a curse felt to be forceful enough to need euphemisms such as *Blame it, Blister it* and *Rasted* (for blasted).

Blast my Timbers, My Bloomin Peepers
U.S. elaborations of above.

Blazes
In oaths, dates from the early 19th century, in combinations such as *Go to blazes, What the blazes, Blazes Kate.* A useful euphemism because it combines the satisfying sound of *Blast* with the sense of *Hell.*

Bletchley Hunt
Rhyming slang. C.f. *Berk*.

Blimey
Cockney word meaning *Blind me*.

Blimey O'Reilly
Elaboration on *Blimey* supposed to be a corruption of *Blind O'Reilly*, a docker and trade unionist famous in Liverpool folk-lore.

Blind me
See *Blimey*.

Blood, S'blood, By the Blood of Christ
The last was the earliest oath, and not a trifling one, but it was already trivialised by the 14th century. According to Chaucer a poor throw of the dice was enough to prompt gamesters to '*By the blood of Christ that is in Hayles*'. (A phial of Christ's blood was believed to be preserved at Hayles, Glos.) Shortened to *S'blood* the oath was popular with Elizabeth and her court. Later gallants favoured combinations such as *Blood and oons* and *Blood and thunder*.

(My) Blood Oath
Current Australian oath.

Bloody
Or the case of the swear word that never was.
This adjective, with no previous obscene or blasphemous associations, became in 19th century England one of the great taboos of the language. It's a prime example of English middle-class hypocrisy. *Bloody*'s only crime was that it became non-U.
In the latter half of the 18th century the word lost caste. (Earlier it had been rather O.K. and upper middle.) Once it became established as a nasty working-class word the philologists got busy with explanations. Some said it was a contraction of *By our Lady*, others that it was a shortening of the earlier *S'blood* (from *Christ's blood*). Not very satisfactory explanations philologically, and anyway why should *Bloody* be so much worse than all the earlier oaths on the Virgin, on Christ's blood, body, nails and guts, etc? Other suggestions were Celtic, German and Russian origins, also a derivation from the 17th century 'blood' meaning 'young rip'. But the most obvious explanation is the most likely. This is that *Bloody*, originally an adjective meaning 'covered with blood', and hence 'violent', acquired a general pejorative sense. (The playwright Shadwell used it in this sense when he referred in 1668 to the 'bloody hands of the critics'.) Gradually

the word became a rather upper-class intensive, like the modern 'frightfully' and 'awfully'. It still wasn't much of a shocker in 1714 when Dean Swift wrote casually to a female acquaintance 'it was bloody hot walking today'.

In the 18th century both in England and her American colonies, British soldiers were known as 'bloody backs'. Grose, in his dictionary of 1785, explains the nickname as a 'jeering appellation for a soldier, alluding to his scarlet coat', and this is probably an example of the word in transition from U to non-U. In the U.S. just before the War of Independence the colonists had a more literal explanation. They attributed the nickname to the blood from the constant floggings necessary to keep the rascally British soldiers in order.

Throughout the 19th century *Bloody* was one of the working man's hardest working pejoratives, but quite unmentionable in polite society. In 1914 Shaw helped shatter the taboo, when his heroine actually uttered the words '*Not bloody likely*' on stage in PYGMALION. During the Great War the Tommies were as well known abroad for their *Bloody*s as their 14th and 15th century counterparts for their *Goddam*'s (see p. 18). By 1920, with a crop of realistic war novels, the word resurfaced in print.

Bloody has spread the length of the old British Empire, especially to Australia, but not to the U.S.A., where the way the English use the word is regarded as just another quaint English eccentricity.

Bloody end to me, I wish my Bloody eyes may drop out

Oaths of the Victorian underworld, quoted in a 19th century slang dictionary.

Blue

As in *Ginger blue bird, Jumping Moses on a blue raft, Ye Gods and small blue fishes.*

In these assorted oaths *Blue* may simply have been added to give colour, but the word is good value: the initial consonants recall *Bloody* and there are also overtones of risqué jokes and language. (One authority derives this sense from the blue traditionally worn by harlots.) Another possibility is the influence of French oaths such as *Sacrebleu, Morbleu,* where *Bleu* is a euphemism for *Dieu,* god.

Blow it, me up, down, etc.

Euphemism for *Blast.*

Blow off me Last Limb

Old salt's equivalent of 'Cross my heart and hope to die'.

Blurt

16th century equivalent of 'Sucks to you'.

Bob
In oaths such as the Cockney *Swelp me Bob* and the U.S. *No Siree Bob,* is probably a euphemism for *God*. The form *Swelp me Cat* is found where *Cat* is certainly a corruption of *God*. It's less likely that this *Bob* is a corruption of *Babe* i.e. God's babe. But see also *Ods Bobs*.

Bodkins, Ods Bodkins, Ods Boddikins
Now humorous and archaic expressions, once deadly earnest. Corruptions of *God's body* + diminutive -ikins. In 19th century 'flash' or slang another *Bodikin* was also well-known as a contraction of *Bawdy-ken* or brothel, perhaps making the oath a risqué pun for those in the know.

Bollocks
See *Ballocks*.

Boloney, Baloney
Nonsense. Imported from the U.S. Take your pick from traditional derivation from Bologna sausages, made of poor quality meat, hence a load of rubbish, or from a gipsy origin: the Romany word *Pelone* means testicles.

Bots
'*A bots on you*', says the Vicar of Wakefield, in Goldsmith's novel. A rural variant of 'A plague on you'. *Bots* are nasty parasitical worms found in horses' stomachs.

Bounce Tail and God Have Mercy Guts
Strapping Rabelaisian oath from the 17th century.

Bovril
Occasional Australian euphemism for *Bullshit*.

Bozzimacoo
Sounds Italian or South American, but is a Yorkshire tyke's corruption of the French *Baise mon cul,* Kiss my arse.

(By) Bread and Salt
A Tudor oath. It was customary to take bread and salt before swearing a solemn oath.*

Bugger
Originally, to call someone a *Bugger* meant simply that you thought

*Ashley Montagu. THE ANATOMY OF SWEARING.

he was a heretic. The word comes from *Bulgar,* after an 11th century sect of Bulgarian heretics. The sense of pervert was acquired a century or so later from the doings of the Albigensian heretics, renowned throughout Europe for their sexual excesses. The Albigensians believed that life on earth was the work of the devil. So they longed for death and the eternal bliss to follow – but meanwhile why not make life as pleasant as possible?

As a noun used colloquially, the word has always been vulgar, but not necessarily offensive. Dr Johnson defined it as a 'term of endearment between sailors'. In Victorian thieves' slang it had an odd meaning: 'a stealer of breast pins from drunks'.

As an expletive Partridge* records the earliest usage as 1793. Since when, of course, it's been in non-stop active service, in England at least. Now much less shocking than thirty years ago: it was actionable in print before 1934. Like *Bloody* and *Bastard, Bugger* seems to be ruder in England than anywhere else.

(The) Bugs

U.S. early 20th century exclamation of irritation, with echoes of *Bugger*. Possibly of American Irish origin. In the 18th century *Bugs* was the Irish nickname for the English: bugs having been introduced into Ireland by the British, according to best Irish traditions.

Bumfay

See *Bumtroth.*

Bumswizzled, I'll be

A weird U.S. oath from way back in American history. *Swizzle* was an old American drink, a mixture of spruce beer, rum and sugar. It was so good that in 1760 the English regiment stationed at Fort Ticonderoga founded their own *Swizzle* Club, where presumably they got themselves thoroughly *Swizzled*. (In Yorkshire dialect too a *Swizzler* is an old soak.) The first element has nothing to do with the good old English word for bottom. In U.S. slang *Bum* often means 'useless', 'packed-up', as here.

Bumtroth, Bumfay, Bomfay

Common early corruptions of *By my faith, By my troth.* Harmless expressions you might think but in the 17th century one Thomas Buttand was found guilty of swearing and fined for an *On my troth.*

Bungay, Go to

Often *Go to Bungay for a bottom.* Go to hell. Not anatomical. Bungay is a town in Suffolk where boats were repaired.

*Partridge. A DICTIONARY OF SLANG AND UNCONVENTIONAL ENGLISH.

Burn
Originally a dialect alternative for *Go to hell* (and burn). Later used euphemistically, especially in the U.S., for *Damn* and *Darn,* in expressions such as *Gol burn it*, etc.

Bust me
Originally a mild Dickensian oath. Widely used later as an American euphemism for *Blast.*

Buttock of a Monk
A Rabelaisian oath from the 17th century English translation of PANTAGRUEL, featuring an incredibly fluent swearer-extraordinary, Friar John. Most of the best oaths in PANTAGRUEL are literary once-offs, coined specially for the book, and therefore hardly fall in the scope of this Meanings, but PANTAGRUEL is highly recommended reading for enthusiasts.

By Gum
Telescoping of *By God Almighty* or *God save me.* Traditionally the oath of all North Country comics. See also under *Gum.* For other even weirder dialect corruptions of *By God* see *Bedad.*

Cabbage
A theme common to Ancient Greek and modern Australian ejaculations. The Greeks swore by the Cabbage because they prized it as a hangover cure.* The Australian exclamation *My Cabbage tree* refers to the old Aussie trick of making a sun hat out of the leaves of the Cabbage tree, a type of palm.

Cadaver, By my
Over my dead body. Late Victorian Cockney oath.

Caesar's Crutch, Great Caesar's Ghost
Vaguely classical euphemisms, good value because of the phonetic similarity to *Jesus Christ.*

Capot me
An 18th and 19th century imprecation, roughly equivalent to *Stone me.* Derives from the card game Picquet, in which taking all twelve tricks (quite a feat) is called a 'capot'.

Carimari, Carymary
An oath imported from Italy, fashionable in the 16th century. From the Italian *Cara Maria,* or *Dear (Virgin) Mary.*

*Montagu. Op. cit.

Cats

A 17th and 18th century corruption of *God's* in oaths such as *Cats nouns* (*God's wounds*) and *Swelp me Cat*. This could also be the origin of the peculiar *Cat* in the many U.S. expressions such as *Cold Cats, Jiminy whizzlecats, Suffering cat fish, Holy fishcats,* etc.

Caulk me Dead Lights

Blind me. Victorian sailors' oath. Literally: bung up my eyes.

Cheese Cake, Holy, Cheese and Crust, Cheese on Crackers got all Muddy

U.S. punning euphemisms for *Jesus Christ* and *God Almighty*.

(Dead) Chelsea by God

An interesting oath, ascribed to a grenadier at the battle of Fontenoy. He had had his leg blown off by a cannon ball and was therefore sure of being shipped home to the Chelsea Military Hospital.

Christ

In oaths, usually conceded to be a degree stronger than *God: For God's sake* is permissible, *For Christ's sake* less so. Has prompted many euphemisms, mainly 19th century and especially from the U.S., such as *Crikey, Crimes, Criminy, For Crimp's sake, Cripes, Sleeping Cripe, By Crackity, Christmas, Crummy, For crying out loud*. See also *Jesus Christ*.

(By) Cob's Body

An 18th century corruption of *By God's body*.

Cobblers

A load of nonsense. From Cockney rhyming slang. *Cobblers* awls rhymes with *Balls*.

(By) Cock, By Cokkes Bones, By Coks Body

In these early oaths *Cok* is a corruption of *God*.

(By) Cock and Pie

Sounds like a nursery rhyme oath but it was deadly serious in early English and meant *By God and the Ordinal* (the instructions at the beginning of the Prayer Book for the daily order of service).

(By) Cock's Precious Podstick

Strange Elizabethan corruption of *By God's precious body*.

Cock it, A Load of Hot Cock, (You) Cocksucker
A cock from quite another farmyard. In these expressions *Cock* means penis, a sense which goes back at least as far as the early 17th century and maybe earlier. (Cock Lane in Smithfield was notorious as a red light area in the 14th century.*) For a long time the indelicate punning possibilities have been causing embarrassment. Englishmen must be careful how they pronounce 'Cockburn' (to rhyme with 'Woburn'), how they enquire whether they have reached Cockfosters on the Underground. American farmers of seventy years ago mentioned haycocks and weathercocks in polite society at their peril. There's even an apocryphal tale of a young American miss who referred to her brother in the Navy as a 'roosterswain'. Another American, Amos Bronson Alcox, changed his name for reasons of delicacy. This was perhaps just as well for his daughter Louisa Mary. Would any well-brought up little American child of the period have been permitted to read LITTLE WOMEN or GOOD WIVES by L. M. Alco*x*?

Cod, Code, Coad, Cot, Cud
Typically 17th century corruptions of *God* as in *Codsfish* (*God's flesh*), *Cotzooks* (*God's hooks*), *Cots my life* (*kins*) (*God save my life*), *Cuds Nigs* (*God's Nails*). (Only the most naïve can have been unaware of the double pun on *Cod,* both fishy and anatomical, so these oaths were probably often facetious.)

Cods
Rude 17th century nickname for a curate. See *Ballocks.*

Codsfish
See *Cod.*

Cods hooks
God's hooks, or *nails.*

Codswallop
20th century equivalent to *Balderdash.* Whether it's decent or not is hard to say for its origin is obscure. Maybe it just means 'What you've just said is a load of wet flopping fish'. Alternatively it could be a combination of *Cod* meaning scrotum + *Wallop* doing euphemistic duty for *Ballocks.*

Cold puppies, Cats
Weird U.S. quasi-oaths in which *Cold* usually implies vexation, just as *Hot* (in 'hot mastiff', '-puppy', '-sock', '-tabasco') implies approval.

*Peter Aykroyd. EVIL LONDON.

Colonial
Australian *My colonial oath* and *My bloody colonial oath* are often shortened to *My Colonial.*

Confound it
Now a trifle stagey. 17th to 19th century upper class oaths.

Continental, I don't give a
A 19th century U.S. oath. It originated in the War of Independence during which the currency issued by the Continental Congress was practically worthless.

Coo, Coo-er
Traditionally Cockney, abbreviations either of *God* or *Good.* See also *Cor.*

Coo Lummy, Cor Lummy
Cockney forms of *God love me.*

Cor, Cor Blimey, Cor Luv a Duck
The Cockney oaths every foreign tourist expects to hear – and probably will – as he walks down the Strand.

Cork Screw
Victorian substitute for *God's truth.*

Cots my Life (Kins)
See *Cod.*

Cotzooks
See *Cod.*

(By) Crackity
U.S. euphemism for *By Christ.*

Crap
Means shit and perhaps wouldn't be used so lightly were this better known. (In the less permissive days of the 1940s Auntie B.B.C. must have had some sticky moments when J. F. Crapp used to field in the gulley for Gloucester County Cricket team.)

(By) Crickety, Crikey, Crimes, Criminy, Cripes
Some of the most popular substitutes for *Christ,* mostly dating from the 19th century. *Cripes* is one of the oldest, recorded from the 17th century and still current today.

Crippen
Kids' exclamation, a reference to a notorious Edwardian murderer, the one who buried his wife in the cellar and made off to America with his mistress. Made history in 1910 as the first murderer to be picked up through intercontinental radio link.

Crud (You)
Quite as low as some other four-letter words but less used, outside Australia and Canada. Etymologically *Crud* is the same word as 'curd'.

Crumbs, Crummy
Schoolboy comic strip oaths, probably euphemisms for *Christ*. A second possibility is that both derive from Victorian slang, in which *Crummy* meant lousy, so *Crumbs* and *Crummy* could both be straight expressions of disgust.

Cuds Nigs
See *Cod*.

Cunt
Common to most European languages, with similar forms recorded in Egyptian, Greek, Latin, Old Norse and French. It's there in Chaucer's Miller's Tale for all smutty schoolboys to read, but thereafter has made only rare appearances in print: in common with *Fuck* (q.v.) the word was actionable in print till 1960. Of the two *Cunt* seems always to have been slightly the more obscene. Cicero the Roman lawyer recommended in his handbook for other orators that *Cunnus*, the Latin form, should be avoided. Nearly two millenia later Grose, in his DICTIONARY OF THE VULGAR TONGUE, felt the same, printing the word with two asterisks and defining it 'a dirty word for a dirty thing'. Even in James Jones' notoriously oathful modern novel FROM HERE TO ETERNITY, the publishers removed the word entirely from the author's MS (though according to an anonymous teller they left in 108 *Fuck*'s and 50 *Shit*'s).

Curse of Cromwell, Curse of the Crows on ye
Old fingerwagging maledictions recorded from the north of England. Probably Anglo-Irish.

Dad-boggle, -fetch, -gan, -gern, -gorn, -gum, -gun it
Typically U.S. euphemisms, often with consonant switching, for *Goddamm it*, with variants *I'll be dadboggled*, etc. *Dad* and *Dod* were common early English dialect forms of *God*. See also *Dod*.

Daggers, also Diggers, S'diggers
Popular Restoration oaths.

Dagnabbed, I'll be
Way-out U.S. substitute for *I'll be doggoned* (q.v.).

Damn
Almost certainly derives from Latin *Damno,* to punish or condemn, though one way-out theory is a corruption of the old French *Dame* from Latin *Dominus,* used as a euphemism for *God*.
In the 14th and 15th centuries *Goddam* (q.v.) was the most popular form, so much so that English soldiers were known throughout Europe as *Goddams*. Later *Damn* seems to have taken over and become one of the most overworked swearwords of the 17th century, though to keep up with the 'ton' you had to use the correct affected pronunciation. (In 1698 this was 'dem me', not 'dam me', according to one of the fops in a contemporary play.) So notorious were the 17th and 18th century rips for their cursing and swearing that they were nicknamed *Dammeboys*. Grose* refers to them as 'roaring mad, blustering fellows, scourers of the streets, or kickers up of a breeze'. By the late 18th century Bob Acres in Sheridan's RIVALS was sick and tired of the word. '*Damns have had their day*' he says. In the 19th century the Victorians went into their usual contortions to avoid the dreadful word, producing the weirdest corruptions (*Ding, Dang, Dum, Durn, Gun, Dosh,* etc.) and various far-fetched substitutes, (*Gardenia* q.v., *Therewith* q.v., *I'll be bamboozled*). Even in this century spelling was often altered, as in *Damphule,* to get round the taboo.
Acres seems to have been wrong anyway. *Damn*'s are still with us and likely to stay.

Dam(n), I don't give a
The historian Macaulay credited the Duke of Wellington with inventing this oath. A dam was a practically worthless Indian coin, and the Iron Duke served in India as a young soldier. Diverting the derivation may be, but the OXFORD DICTIONARY (and majority opinion) is against it.

Dang
19th century euphemism for *Damn*. Very innocuous. Even the genteel Victorian novelist Mrs Gaskell used it.

Darn, Darnation
Euphemisms for *Damn,* the second mainly U.S.

*A CLASSICAL DICTIONARY OF THE VULGAR TONGUE, 1785.

Dash
Watery Victorian euphemism from the dash in the printed form *D——n.*

Datheit
Anglo-Norman. One of the earliest recorded English oaths. Comes from an old French word meaning grief or misfortune. Found in expressions such as the 14th century *Dayet his nose* – though this does not sound a thunderingly serious oath.

Dear Joy
Another of those oaths used so frequently by Irishmen in the 18th. century that it became a common nickname for them.* See also *Holy Father*.

Death of a Buffle ox
Rabelais again, explosive and expressive. See also *Buttock of a monk.*

Death – and Eternal Tortures, – and Destruction
Restoration oaths.

Dern
U.S. euphemism for *Damn* q.v.

Deuce, Deuce take it, The Deuce I will
In early English oaths *Deus* or *Dewse* was borrowed from the Latin word for God. By a strange shift in meaning the word now has the sense of devil, perdition. Probably the later meaning comes from the deuce or 2 at cards, the lowest possible, therefore the worst possible luck.

Devil
Consigning oneself and others to the devil has been a steady since the 14th century at least. A Rabelaisian variant (17th century) runs '*The devil boil me like a black pudding*'.

Dickens, What the, or Dickings, Dickin
Much earlier than the novelist, in fact positively Shakespearian. A corruption of *Devilkins,* the diminutive of devil. Has a slightly period flavour in England, but is current in Australia where *Dickin,* or *Dicken on* means come off it.

Digswiggered, I'll be
See *Swiggered.*

*Grose. op. cit.

Dines, By God's
An old English oath. *Dines* is probably from Norman French *Dignesse* or dignity.

Dingbat it
U.S. euphemism for *Goddamn it.* Not to be confused with Anzac *Dingbats* which are D.T.s.

Ding-bust, -swaggle, -swoggle it
More U.S. way-out euphemisms for *Goddamn it.*

Dod
Corruption of *God* in U.S. oaths such as *Dod burn it, Dod souse the luck.*

Dog
In early oaths such as *By Dog's precious wounds Dog* stands for *God* by a kind of euphemistic back slang.

Dog, Damned or Cursed
Compare the French *Sacré chien.* A rarely heard but ancient oath, going back to Roman times. The worst throw in a Roman poker game was the *Canis,* or dog, which Ovid the Latin poet called the *Damnosi canes,* the damned dogs.

Doggone it, I'll be Doggoned
Perversions of *Goddamn it,* etc., probably the best established of all the many U.S. euphemisms. Perhaps the form owes something to the early euphemism *Dog* for *God* (see above).

Drabbit
Dialect version of *Drat it* (q.v.).

Drat it
A mild seeming oath, but the original (*G*)*od rot it* could not be taken so lightly.

(Mrs) Duckett
Rhyming slang and euphemism, as is the Cockney *Do I duck.*

Durn
U.S. corruption of *Damn* (q.v.).

Ecastor, Edepol
Roman equivalents to our *Good Lord.* Castor and Pollux were the

Heavenly Twins, sons of Jove. As a reward for their devotion to each other Jove placed them among the stars as Gemini.

Eck, Ecky
See *Heck.*

Ecod, Egad, Egadlins, Edad
Corruptions of *By God. Egadlins* is an 18th and 19th century diminutive.

Elevens, By the
A Restoration oath. Probably *By the eleven disciples.*

(My) eye(s), (All) my eye and Betty Martin
The modern *My eye* expresses mild disbelief, probably abbreviated from an earlier *Damn my eye(s).* The *Betty Martin* elaboration may be the remains of a serious oath. One ingenious explanation is that it is a corruption of *O mihi, beate Martine,* a Latin prayer meaning Help me Saint Martin.

(Damn my) eyes, limbs and blue breeches
Traditionally the hardest used oath of 18th century footguards. It earned them the nickname of 'the eyes and limbs'.*

F.A., Sweet
In the Navy, Fanny Adams used to be slang for boiled mutton, a sick joke if ever there was one, for the original Fanny was murdered, dismembered and dumped in a river at the beginning of the 19th century. As there wasn't much left of her *Sweet F.A.* came to mean sweet nothing. (But of course the initials can represent other words. As the reader pleases.)

Fackin(g)s, By my fac, Fait, Faix, Fey, Fecks, Fegs, Yfacks
All early corruptions of *Faith, By my faith.*

Fart
An ancient vulgarity, onomatopeic in origin, like the French *Péter.* (A particularly noisy firework is still called a *Pétard* in French.) The word was used by the best authors; a typical Ben Jonson insult was '*I fart at thee*'. Indeed Jonson even included the word in his court masques for James I. (Like other vulgarisms, *Fart* has inspired various slangy compounds and swear words, not generally repeatable, as for example the 17th century *Cackling-fart* or egg, and 18th century *Fart-catcher* or footman, 'from his following behind his master'.*)

*Grose. op. cit.
*Grose. op. cit.

Feather me
Australian oath. Perhaps an abbreviation of *Tar and feather me*.

(The) Ferrups take you, What the Ferrups
What the *Ferrups* were is quite obscure. An old Lancashire and Yorkshire dialect oath.

Fiddlesticks
Refined 19th century exclamation used by Victorian ladies. Not as innocent as its users: in contemporary low slang *Fiddlestick* meant penis.

Fie (on you)
Now archaic and mocking. Used in the sense *Devil take you* by Malory and Chaucer. Literally: stinks to you. Comes via Norman French from the Latin *Fi,* which the Romans would exclaim when holding the nose at a bad smell.

(A) Fig for, By my fig, -figgins, By hard figs, Fig's end
All these expressions, and the modern *Not to care a fig for,* probably derive from the 16th century insult *Fico to you* with accompanying gesture. To make the Spanish Fig was to stick the thumb out between the first two fingers, with obvious sexual symbolism.

Flaming Hanovers
An oath said to be local to Liverpool, and to refer to an unpopular Hanoverian regiment stationed there. See also *Go to Hanover*.

Flesh and Fire
Variant of the popular 16th to 18th century *S'flesh* and *God's flesh.*

Footer, Footy, (my) Foot
The modern *My foot* is mild enough, but the Victorian *Foot* probably derived from the French *Fous-moi le camp,* and was a pretty rude injunction to clear off. From the same French verb came several dialect words, all contemptuous, but by no means taboo, such as *Footy, Foutiness,* and *Fouter*. Most are obsolete, but if you were time-wasting in Lancashire or Yorkshire today, you might still be accused of *Footering about*. The same *Footy* is common in West Indian. E.G. '*You footy well have to pay me*'.

France, What De Bloomin
Used by West Indians as a euphemism for *Hell*. A vestige of French colonial unpopularity?

Friar
Rhyming slang and euphemism rolled into one, in expressions such as *Run like the good friar* with *Tuck* understood. (Thanks to D. Bogle.)

Fricking
Euphemism from the combination of *Fucking* and *Frigging*.

Frig it, Frig pig, Frigging
The 18th century compound *Frig pig* was a 'trifling, fiddle-faddle fellow'* but the simple verb is not to be trifled with: since the 16th century at least it has meant to masturbate. The expletive *Frig it* is fairly recent, as is *Frigging* as a rude intensive.

Fuck (it), Fucking
An ancient crudity with roots in Latin and Celtic. Appearances in dictionaries, let alone literature, have been rare. One of the earliest instances of the word may be a 13th century reference to one John Le Fucker. Carl Darling Buck, the philologist who unearthed this example, derives the name from *Fyke* or *Fike* meaning to fidget, which at least gives the poor man the benefit of the doubt.
Dr Johnson left the word out of his DICTIONARY, as did most of his successors till Partridge's prodigious DICTIONARY OF SLANG in 1936. Since the Lady Chatterley case in 1960, when for the first time Lawrence's book was published unexpurgated, it has been legally permissible in this country to spell out the word in full in print. It now appears in most modern dictionaries and has been heard on television and radio, even on one occasion on the B.B.C.'s respectable WOMAN'S HOUR.
(Common euphemisms are: *Furk, Furking, Muck, Mucking, Flip, Flipping, Frick, Fricking, Mrs Duckett, Frair Tuck.*)

Fudge
An 18th century in-word for Nonsense. (A character in Goldsmith's VICAR OF WAKEFIELD keeps interrupting the conversation with *Fudge,* to the Vicar's great irritation.) All sorts of derivations have been suggested, among them an earlier verb meaning to forge or counterfeit and a Gaelic word for a practically worthless coin. The most colourful but least plausible derivation is from the exploits of one Captain *Fudge, a* 17th century merchantman commander. His seamanship was suspect but not his salesmanship, and at the end of each voyage he would tell whoppers about the excellence of his cargo. Hence perhaps *Fudge,* an exaggeration or lie?

Gad, Gar, Ged, Gud
Common corruptions of *God*.

*Grose. op. cit.

Gadsbodikins
By God's body + diminutive *-kins*.

Gads bud, Budlikins
By God's blood + diminutive *-likins*.

Gads me, Gads my life
Short for *God save me* or *my life*.

Gadso
A 17th to 19th century oath. Though Dickens has a very respectable undertaker exclaim *Gadso,* the oath was probably not at all respectable. According to earlier dictionaries *Gadso* comes from the Italian *Cazzo* or penis.

Gadsobs
God's tears.

Gadsooks, Gadzooks
Gods' hooks or *nails*. 17th and 18th century oaths. Nowadays a typical stage oath for the Bad Baron and a favourite with dramatists aiming at an ersatz period flavour.

Gammon
Bosh, nonsense. Often in the combinations *All smoke, gammon and pickles,* or *Gammon and spinach,* which are deliberate or accidental puns on the two senses of *Gammon* ('ham' and 'game'). From a 17th century verb meaning to con, trick, or play games with. (The *Gammon* in backgammon is the same word.)

Gardenia
Disguised spelling of the U.S. euphemism *God deen you* (or *damn you*).

Garn(it)
In the U.S. just another substitute for *Damn*. In England *Garn* is more an angry inarticulate growl than a word, with the clear message, 'scram', 'push off'.

Gawblimey
Cockney for *God blind me*. See *Blimey*.

Gaw, Gawd, Gawd Aggie, Gawd luv a duck
Cockney and Australian pronunciation of *God: Aggie* and *Luv a duck* are Strine embellishments.

Gawdfer
20th century shortening of *God forbid.*

Gee
Traditionally U.S. Either an abbreviation of *Jesus,* or the pronunciation of the *G* of *God.*

Geekus Crow
U.S. again. Thin disguise for *Jesus Christ.*

Geemud
U.S. euphemistic oath, now old-fashioned. Perhaps the *Mud* is borrowed from *For the love of Mud* where it stands for God.

Gees and Rice
West Indian euphemism for *Jesus Christ.*

Gee Whiz
Probably a euphemism for a long drawn out pronunciation of *Jesus.* Has inspired some particularly fatuous elaborations such as *Gee-Whillicats, -Whillikins, -Whiskers, -Whittakers.*

Gemini, Geminetti, Giminy
Euphemisms for *Jesus. Gemini* appears in the 17th century, the others later. The origin may be telescoping of the Latin *Iesu domine.* See also *Jiminy.*

Geranium(s)
Another flowery U.S. euphemism, like *Gardenia.*

Gerry Gan
Ripe 16th century vulgarism, expressed in contemporary thieves' cant. Literally: *A turd in your mouth.*

Get Knotted
Usage seems to have softened this explicit instruction to *Fuck off.* The expression is widely current. There is even a boutique in the West End called *Get Knotted* (hardly welcoming to prospective clients).

Get Stuffed
Graphic metaphor from the upholstery trade. If you prefer to be genteel, substitute the R.A.F. version *Go and see a taxidermist.*

(By) Gigs
As used in the 16th and 17th centuries, rather an innocuous silly oath. Either *By my nose* or by association with *Gog* corrupted from *God*. But see also *Giggy*.

(Up your) Giggy
Modern Canadian equivalent of 'you know where you can put it'. An interesting survival of a word now practically obselete in England. *Gigg* in 18th and 19th century English meant 'a nose, a high one-horse chaise, and a woman's privities'.*

(By) Gilliver, By Jilly
More U.S. euphemisms for *Jesus*.

Gimpson root, Thunder and
Strange early 20th century oath from the U.S., on the pattern of the many German immigrant oaths such as *Donner und Blitzen*. *Gimpson root* is almost certainly a corruption of *Ginseng root*. (*Panax Ginseng* is a plant found in China, Korea and North America. Its aromatic root was valued highly by Chinese mandarins for its medicinal qualities). It is still used by Mexican Indians to induce euphoria in 'magic medicine'. It is considered a potent aphrodisiac.

(By) Gis, Jis
Early forms of *Jesus*. Shakespeare's Ophelia swore '*By Gis and by Saint Chanty*'. Possibly the form arose from the common Greek abbreviation (the first three letters of *Jesus*), but it's more likely to be a casual shortening of the same word, as in the later U.S. *Jeeze*.

Go to hell
Has countless elaborations and euphemisms from the early *Go shake your ears* (recorded in 1573), *God teach your grannum -to crack filberds, -to grope ducks, -to such sour milk,* to the later *Go and take a carrot, Go and eat coke (and shit cinders),* and the West Indian *Man go wash your skin. Go to hell – and pump thunder – and help your mother make a bitch pie*. See also under *Bungay, Bath, Halifax* and *Hoboken*.

God
Of the various corruptions of *God, Cock* and *Gog* are the earliest (15th to 17th century), *S', Z', Cod, Cat, Cud, Od, Ad Ud, Gad, Ged,* and *Gud* are 17th to 19th century. The only one still heard (occasionally) is *Gad*.

*Grose. op. cit.

In medieval times oaths on various parts of God's body were common. Richard I swore *By God's legs,* Lackland *By God's teeth.* Other favourites were *God's foot, guts, hat* (*heart*), *lik,* and *nigs* (nails).
(Some of the commonest euphemisms and substitutes are: *Ding, Dod, Dog, Godfrey, Gol, Gom, Gosh, Hot.*)

God-a-mercy, God-a-mercy horse
The first is a 16th to 18th century oath, without much force. The second peculiar form is probably a corruption of *God have mercy upon us* – in the mid-17th century it was 'a byword thorou London', according to a contemporary source.

Goddamn (it)
Because of their uninhibited swearing British soldiers in the 15th century were known up and down Europe as the *Goddams,* and Joan of Arc even promised her French troops *Goddams for supper.* Later the Puritans referred to the Cavaliers as *Goddammees.* Today *Goddamn* and *Goddamn it* as expletives are chiefly U.S.

God's Nigs
An early English workaday oath which is ambiguous in English. It could refer either to Christ's fingernails, or the nails of the Cross. The origin may have been an old French oath *Par les cloux Dieu* (meaning iron nails) but probably most early English swearers thought they were referring to finger nails – if they ever thought about it at all.

Goddy's Dome
By God's punishment. Goddy's is an old form of the genitive case.

Gog's Malison, Gog's Wouns
More early English oaths. *Malison* is an old word for curse, *Wouns* a corruption of *Wounds.*

(By) Goles, Golly
By Goles is an early English euphemism (for *God*) but the Victorian *Golly* was probably imported from America, where negroes used it in the 18th century.

(By) Gollation, Gollyopulus
U.S. exclamations of surprise, built on *Golly* (see above).

Good Lack-a-day, Good Lack-a-daisy
The second is a lower class corruption of the first. Female oaths of the 17th and 18th centuries.

Good Lorjusdeys, Goodlorjus o'me
Early North Country oaths. (Recorded 1770.)

Good strange
One of the milder Restoration oaths. Perhaps a corruption of *God's strings?*

(My) Goody
Victorian belowstairs for *My goodness*.

Goodyear take you, what the Goodyear
16th and 17th century expletives. *Goodyear* as a euphemism for syphilis, probably from the French *Gouge,* a camp follower.

Goosh
West Indian version of *Gosh* (q.v.).

Goramity
Negro corruption of *God Almighty*.

Gorblimey
Cockney expletive. Corruption of *God blind me*. The *Gorblimey trousers* Lonnie Donnegan sang about in the 1950's were so loud and flashy that they were supposed to provoke the exclamation.

Gordelpus
Not only a Cockey oath run together but also Victorian low slang for any tramp who sponged around hospital casualty wards.

Gordmekmorning
In Trinidad and Tobago this is an expression of utter exasperation.

Gorm, Be Gormed
Lower class Victorian version of *Goddamn,* etc. A favourite with Dickens' working class characters for instance. Also West Indian.

Gosh
Corruption of *God* recorded early in England, but probably re-imported from the U.S. in Victorian times.

Gosh all -potomac, -hemlock, -fishooks
U.S. comic strip style oaths, recorded in the 19th century.

Gosh blank it, Gosh ding it
U.S. euphemisms for *God damn it*.

Gotterdammerung
Wince-making Victorian punning oath on the Wagnerian opera.

Grease us twice
Neat rhyming euphemism for *Jesus Christ.* (It's not only Cockneys and Australians who indulge in rhyming slang.)

Great
Characteristically U.S. element in a series of rather lightweight oaths such as *Great Barnum, Great goldfish, By the great hornspoon.*

Great Scott, Great Scotland Yard
Originally a U.S. expression, after General Winfield Scott, soldier and presidential nominee, who never made it to the Presidency. When the expression infiltrated English English it was either taken to refer to Sir Walter Scott, or further elaborated into *Great Scotland Yard.*

Greens, S'elp my
Victorian lower class slangy oath, on the pattern of *Swelp me Bob* (q.v.) but not the harmless euphemism it appears, for *Greens* is slang for sex. (Compare *What's the price of greens?*)

Gum, Gummy, Holy Gumdrops
Gum is either a corruption by telescoping of *God Almighty,* or of *God save me.* A stock North Country oath, *Gum* has also travelled a fair bit. By *Gum, Gummy* and *Holy Gumdrops* are American oaths, and *Gum* is also good Strine.

(By the) Hali(g)dom(e)
One of the earliest of English oaths. In Anglo-Saxon times oaths were sworn on *Haligdoms,* or holy relics, and this is probably the origin of the later formula *By God and the holy dam,* traditionally an oath of the Round Table Knights. The same custom was in operation when Harold was tricked into swearing fealty to William of Normandy, over some sacred bones.

Halifax, Go to
19th century euphemism for *Go to Hell,* Probably derived from the much older proverb *From Hell, Hull and Halifax Good Lord deliver us.* In the medieval wool town of Halifax anyone who stole goods worth 13½d or more was executed on the same day and his case only examined afterwards. In the U.S. the expression, probably originally from the British proverb, may well have referred later to Halifax,

Nova Scotia, where many of the unpopular loyalists took refuge after the War of Independence.

Hang (it), Go Hang, etc.
A steady (good Chaucerian and 20th century) and totally respectable expletive.

Hanover, Go to
Originally a Jacobite oath, probably in general use in the 18th century. There was also a Suffolk elaboration *Go to Hanover and hoe turnips* reflecting the general poor opinion of the Hanoverian monarchy. See also *Flaming Hanovers*.

(My) Hat
Mild, rather silly expression, perhaps an abbreviation of *I'll eat my hat,* in its turn possibly an adaptation of the much older *To eat old Rowley's hat.* Old Rowley was Charles II.

Heavens to Betsy
U.S. mild oath of surprise. Maybe a relation of the Betty in *All my eye and Betty Martin* (q.v.)?

Heck, By heck, Eck, Go to ecky
Respectable Lancashire oaths, probably euphemisms of *Hell,* now obsolete. The variant *Will he (I) eckus loike* can still be heard.

H E Double Toothpicks
U.S. verbal hieroglyph, euphemism, for *Hell.*

Helen Maria
Hell and Maria. Punning oath from the U.S. Another on the same lines is *Go to Helen B. Happy.*

Hell and combinations
From the 17th century *Come Hell and the devil, By Hell and brimstone, Hell and damnation, Hell and confusion,* from the 19th, *Hellfire, rape and sodomy,* a few examples from the many combinations. *O Hell* is a pretty lightweight oath these days, but not so long ago *'O Hell',* the family card game, was carefully listed in some card game compendiums as *'O Well.* See also *Go to Hell.*

Hell and Tommy
Modern Australian expletive, probably from the British idiom *To play Hell and Tommy with.* This was possibly a corruption of a much

older *To play Hal and Tommy with,* referring to Henry VIII and Thomas Cromwell and the Dissolution of the Monasteries.

Hell's Bells, Blazes, Mint, Sweat
U.S. and colonial variants.

'Hell!' said the Duchess . . .
An oath popular during World War I, leaving tacitly understood a variety of mishaps to the Duchess's anatomy.

(By) Hick, By Hickory, By Heckelum
Probably all U.S. variations on *By heck* (q.v.) but *By hickory* may be a genuinely old American exclamation. The word was first recorded in Virginia in the 17th century in the form *Pokickery* from the Indian word *Pawcohiccora,* which was the milk pressed from pounded hickory kernels.*

Highgate oath
At certain pubs in Highgate, London, 18th century travellers had to swear a nonsense oath over a pair of horns fastened on to a stick. The oath was 'never to kiss the maid if the mistress was around, never to drink mild beer if stronger was available', and other similar clauses. *Sworn in at Highgate* came to mean sharp or shrewd.

Hlebeshako
Your mother's ears. For some reason a deadly insult among the South African Xoxa tribe. (Thanks to P. Klarer.)

Hoboken, Go to
U.S. euphemism for *Go to Hell.* From *Hoboken,* New Jersey.

Holy and combinations
A long established form of oath, still going strong in the U.S. and Ireland, less so in England. Some favourite U.S. examples are: *Holy cats, -cow, -doughnuts, -gee, -kicker, -pickerel, -pipers, -shit, -show, -smoke, -snooks* (for *Spooks* or saints).

Holy Father
An Irish oath, and once so frequently used by Irish butcher boys (and 'other Irish blackguards', says Grose†) that it was a common nickname for them in the 18th century.

*Mathews. DICTIONARY OF AMERICANISMS.
†op. cit.

Holy Mackerel
A 16th century Rabelaisian and 20th century comic strip oath. Not as infantile as it sounds perhaps. *Mackerel* is slang for a pimp.

(By) The Holy Poker (And Tumbling Tom)
A 19th century Anglo-Irish oath. The *Old poker* was the devil.

Honest injun
U.S. schoolboyish oath, late 19th century. A favourite with Tom Sawyer and Huck Finn. Equivalent to the British (old-fashioned) *Honour bright.*

Hongum
Early Lancastrian version of *Hang it.*

(By) Hooky
Not true, it won't happen. Short for *Hooky Walker,* after one John Walker, who according to a 19th century source was a hook-nosed spy and fluent liar.

(By the) Horn and Hoofe
A 17th century butcher's oath.

Horseshit
Nonsense. Chiefly U.S. Often used to be disguised as *Horse collar, Horse radish,* etc.

Hot almighty, Hot diggety dogetty, Hot diggety damn
U.S. euphemisms in which *Hot* stands for *God.*

Hully gee
Alternative spelling of *Holy gee.*

Icod, Idad, Igodlin, Iggodil
Early corruptions and dialect forms of *By God.*

Jabers, By
See under *Bejabers.*

Jeepers Creepers
Jesus Christ. Brought over to England in World War II by American G.I.s, together with the memorable refrain:

'*Jeepers Creepers,*
Where d'ya get those peepers?'

Jeeze
19th century euphemism for *Jesus,* c.f. *Gis* and *Jis.*

Jerusalem Slim
U.S. euphemism for *Jesus.*

Jesus Christ
Always one of the strongest profanities. The need for substitutes prompted many inventive euphemisms during the 19th century, especially in the U.S., such as *Cheese and crust, Grease us twice,* etc.

Jesus wept
20th century oath, which gained some currency after an off-the-record lapse by the late Richard Dimbleby, the much respected T.V. commentator.

Jigger it, I'll be jiggered (Brit.), Holy jigger (U.S.)
Euphemisms probably formed by a deliberate mixing of *Bugger* and *Jesus.* There may be an echo of Victorian low slang, in which *Jigger* meant penis.

Jiminy cricket or cracket
Substitute for *Jesus Christ.* Immortalised by Disney's famous cartoon cricket who was the voice of Pinocchio's conscience. (*Jimmy whizzle-cats* is an even more fanciful elaboration.) See also *Gemini.*

Jimswizzled, Jimjammed, I'll be
Early 20th century U.S. oaths. The *Jimjams,* or *Jimmies,* was an attack of D.T.s. See also *Bumswizzled.*

(By) Jingo
First appeared in the 17th century as a nonsense word in conjurer's patter, later was used as an oath. It may have been a corruption of a Basque word for *God,* introduced into English by hardswearing Basque harpoonists on whaling ships. In 1878 it gained its particular chauvinistic flavour from the refrain of a popular music-hall song:

'We don't want to fight, but *By Jingo* if we do,
We've got the ships, we've got the men, and got the money too'.

Henceforth the sabre-rattlers (mainly Beaconsfield supporters) ready to go to war with Russia were dubbed *Jingos* and the oath particularly associated with them.

Jis
See *Gis.*

John Browned, I'll be
U.S. for *I'll be Goddamned.*

Jumping -Moses on a blue raft/in a Benzine Buggy, -geraniums, -jellybeans, -jehosophat
The initial J always recalls *Jesus*. Some of these dotty U.S. euphemisms are very expressive and inventive.

Knickers
Popular expletive of the 1970s, probably from the catchphrase *Don't get yer knickers in a twist*. An English expletive but an American word, dating back to the days of the first Dutch settlers of New York, known as the Knickerbockers because this was the name of the short gathered breeches they wore.

La
Started off in the 16th century as a rather aristocratic exclamation, but gradually lost caste, probably because of confusion with serving maids' *Lawks* and *Law* (q.v.).

(By our) Lady, Birladie, Belakin
An early oath on the Virgin found in various forms in the 15th and 16th centuries. (Apparently still current among Shropshire farmers less than 100 years ago.)

Lan(d) Sakes, Good Land, My Land
19th century, mainly lower class oaths. In English dialects *Land* was a corruption of *Lord*.

Llanferfechan Hell
Euphemism of a euphemism; all the Fs in the Welsh town here stand for *Effing*.

Lawk, Lauk, Lawks, Lawkamussy, Lawkadaisy
Low Victorian (female) euphemisms for *Lord*. *Lawkamussy* is a corruption of *Lord have mercy*, *Lawkadaisy* of *Lack a day*.

(By the) Laws, Lawsy, Lawsa me, Lawsamassa
Law is a euphemism for *Lord*. *By the Laws* appeared in the 18th century, the other forms were later and common in slovenly Victorian and U.S. negro speech. UNCLE TOM'S CABIN is full of *Laws* and *Lawsamassa*.

Leerodies
Irish equivalent to *Balls*. (Thanks to G. S. Rickards of Shooters Hill.)

Lord Aggie
Modern Australian oath. Tagging on Christian names to oaths is a favourite Australian trick. C.f. *Blimey Charlie* and *Teddy*.

Lord Harry, By the
Lord Harry was a Restoration nickname for the devil.

(For the) Love of Mike, Mud, Pete, etc., for all loves
Here *Mike, Mud* and *Pete,* etc., are modern euphemisms for *God* and *Christ*. *For all loves* is a much older oath, recorded in the 14th century, and rather aristocratic and ladylike (though it does sound as if it should have been Casanova's oath).

Mack, Mackins, (By the)
Early, rather uncouth corruptions of *Marry* or *Mary*.

Marry come up, Marry gep, Marry muff
All are oaths on the *Virgin Mary,* plus various dialect tags of little meaning. (A further elaboration *Marry come up, my dirty cousin* is an old rural catchphrase addressed to someone putting on too many airs and graces.)

(By the) Mass, Maskins, Bithmass, Bithmaskins
An old English oath presumably more relevant before Henry VIII's Act of Supremacy, but the forms *Bithmass* and *Bithmaskins* were common in Lancashire as late as the 18th and 19th centuries.

Meggins. Megsty me
As Meg is Scottish for Mary, so these are Scottish forms of *Mack* and *Mackins* (q.v.).

Mighty (me), Mighty be owers
Quaint dialect corruptions especially Scottish, of (*Al*)*mighty* (*God*).

Mihercle
Common Roman oath. Hercules was the strongman hero of classical mythology.

Mist all crikey, Myst all critey
U.S., Australian and New Zealand euphemisms by deliberate spoonerism.

(Your) Moer
Go to hell. A strongly offensive Afrikaans oath, insulting a man through his mother.

Moses, Holy, By the holy jumping mother of Moses, By the Piper that played before Moses
Perhaps the simple reason why it's always *Moses* who pops up in these predominantly U.S. oaths – rather than Abraham, Elijah or any of the other prophets – is that the initial consonant offers the best value for oaths and exclamations.

Mother
Oh mother referring to one's own mother after some mild calamity is innocuous enough, but of all oaths the direct references to someone else's mother are usually among the strongest and coarsest. In the modern U.S. *You mother* the four-letter verb is omitted but the incestuous implication is clear.

Mud, Gee
See under *Geemud*.

Muggeridge
Quoted by a B.B.C. Woman's Hour listener as her favourite expletive for moments of extreme irritation. After Malcom Muggeridge of course.

Murrain, What a
An Elizabethan alternative for *What the plague*. *A murrain* was a cattle disease.

Nails
Early abbreviation of *God's nails*. See *Neaks* below.

Nation
Frequent 18th century abbreviation of *Damnation,* both in the U.S. and in English dialects. Often used as an emphatic adjective, as in *A nation long way,* and held to be rather vulgar at the time. Grose* complained that this usage was particularly rife in the Home Counties. See also *Tarnation* and *Tarnal*.

Neaks, Neagues
Old oaths, corruptions of *God's nigs* or nails.

Nerts
Slightly more polite than *Nuts* of which it is a (faintly) disguised pronunciation.

Newgate seize me
A 19th century underworld oath, and not a light one. Until pulled

*Grose. A CLASSICAL DICTIONARY OF THE VULGAR TONGUE.

down in 1902 Newgate was a most dreaded prison. Built in the 15th century, it was twice burnt down, once in the Great Fire of 1666 and again in the Gordon Riots of 1780. The Old Bailey now stands on the site of Newgate.

Nick me
Slangy 18th century curse with the same meaning as today: catch (or arrest) me unawares.

Nick take me
This time *Nick* is the devil.

Niggers noggers
Nothing to do with racial prejudice or stewed prunes (R.A.F. slang for which was *Niggers knackers*) but a jocular elaboration on the 17th century oath *Nigs* (from *God's nigs* or nails).

Nouns
Minced 17th century form of *God's wounds*.

Nuts
Nonsense. Chiefly U.S. and Canadian. *Nuts* and nutmegs have been low slang for testicles since the 17th century at least.

Oath, My Kin(g), My blood oath
Popular Strine oaths. *Kin* is a polite abbreviation of a longer verbal form.

Od, Ods
This corruption of *God's* is the first element in many strange sounding oaths, (see below) and was particularly common in Restoration dramatists such as Farquhar and Otway, as well as in many dialect forms.

Ods belly
Ods blastnastum. Weird version from the Isle of Wight.
Odsbobs. Corruption of *God's body* or *babe*.
Odsbobs and buttycakes. A Lancashire elaboration.
Ods bodkins. See *Bodkins*.
Odds dos and dodges. A meaningless Victorian variant.
Ods firkin. Jocular nautical oath. A *Firkin* is a small barrel, half the size of a *Kilderkin* (see below).
Ods fish. *God's flesh*.
Ods guts and gizard.
Ods-hang-leet-on-one. Strange example from Westmorland.
Ods heartlikins. *God's little heart*.

Ods kilderkins. Presumably twice as weighty as *Ods firkin* (q.v.).
Ods life. Abbreviation of *As God's my life*.
Ods nigs/niggers. God's nails.
Ods pittikins. *God's pity*. A Shakespearian oath.
Ods plut and her nails. 18th century Welsh oath.
Odd rabbit it. 18th century corruption of *God rot it*. (The same expression as Modern English *Drat it*.)
Odds my timbers. Early version of the standard naval oath.
Odso. Abbreviation of *God's soul*.
Odspittkins. Scottish version of *God's pity*. (From Fife.)
Odsooks. *God's hooks*, or *nails*.

O. Henry
Literary-minded New Yorkers' substitute for *Oh Hell*. Early 20th century. After O. Henry the short story writer.

Oons
Very popular minced form of *God's wounds*. 17th and 18th century.

Packets
Rather watery Victorian exclamation of surprise or incredulity. In the 18th century a *Packet* was a false report.

Paff
A rude 18th century interjection.

Pappayo
Modern West Indian exclamation of incredulity, usually accompanied by shrieks of laughter. It has a fascinating ancestry, going right back via Spanish and Latin to the Greek παπαιάξ, (*Papai ax*). In Greek tragedy, *Papai* was the traditional exclamation of pain as the dagger sank into your heart, (or your cry of dismay when you heard that your ten children, wife and father-in-law had been killed at the sack of Troy, etc.) In Greek comedy characters often mocked the histrionics of the more serious plays, using the burlesque form *Papaiax* – whence, presumably, the modern West Indian form.

Pardee
Anglicised from the French *Par Dieu, By God,* in Norman times. A very mild oath.

Parliament, Kiss my
An old version of a wellworn insult. According to Pepys's diary for February 1660 the rude boys who shouted it on that day were referring to the Rump Parliament.

Pash, By God's
By God's Passion, the sufferings of Christ on the Cross. A forceful early oath.

Pax
See *Pox.*

Peacock, Oaths on the
In the 13th and 14th centuries when the courtly code of chivalry was most strictly observed, it was the custom to take formal oaths at banquets, over the body of the bird. Before a particularly solemn undertaking this might be a peacock or a swan. Edward I took the Vows of the Swan in 1306, when knighting his son before invading Scotland. Edward III took the Vows of the Heron in 1338 before invading France.

Pease, What a
See *Pie, Pies.*

Peepers, Blast my bloomin
U.S. World War II for *Damn my eyes.*

Phooey
U.S. plagiarism of the German *Pfui,* shame on you, presumably borrowed from German immigrants.

Pickers and stealers, By these
By these hands. From a slang expression found as early as Shakespeare and only recently obsolete. The reference is to the promise in the Catechism (which once upon a time all good children learnt by heart) 'to keep my hands from picking and stealing'.

Pie, Pies take him, A pize on . . ., Pease, Poise
17th and 18th century maledictions, probably derived from *Poison,* which affected beaux may have pronounced 'pisun'.

Piff, Paff, Puff
All meant *Nonsense.* All possibly derived from *Piffle,* by back-formation. Obsolete in England for some time but heard in the U.S. in the early 20th century nonsense oath *Piff and suffering sea-serpents.*

Pigs
Pigs to you is an Australian insult, with an oblique reference to the dirty conditions in which pigs are supposed to be happy.

Pink
Often does duty for *Bloody,* as in *The pink limit* and *Strike me pink.*

Pish
Popular 17th and 18th century exclamation of contempt. For example, '*Pish*' said Sir Thomas Blodworth, Lord Mayor of London, one hour after the Great Fire of London had started, '*A woman could piss it out*'. Probably a corruption of *God's flesh.*

Piss
Till the end of the 18th century the word in its functional sense was not a vulgarism. (See the preceding quote.) As a pithy swear word it was a favourite of Restoration gallants. In his dictionary of 1785 Grose felt quite free to print the word without asterisks, and to add the neatly apposite couplet:

'He who once a good name gets
May piss-a-bed and say he sweats.'

20th century initialising (*P.O.* (*Q.*) for *Piss Off Quickly,* etc.) shows that polite society is still as hung up as the Victorians were about body functions. See also *Shit, piss and corruption.*

Pize, What a
See *Pie.*

Plague, What a
Must have been a pretty forceful oath until memories of the great epidemics of the Black Death had faded.

Pody Cody
Extraordinary 17th century oath, possibly a corruption of *Body of God.*

Pol, By the
Short for *Pollux,* one of the Heavenly Twins. (The other half was Castor.) A Renaissance oath, when classical references were the rage.

Pon rep
Telescoping of *Upon my reputation.* Used in 17th and 18th century aristocratic circles.

Porthors, By this
Strange-looking Chaucerian oath. A *Porthors* was a medieval prayer-book which could easily be carried (French *porter*) outside (French *hors*).

Pox, Pax on it, What the pox
One of James I's favourite oaths, very common from the 16th to

the 19th century. Not smallpox or chickenpox but syphilis, from the *Pocks* or pustules of the disease. Traditionally syphilis was introduced to Europe by Columbus's sailors on their return from Haiti in 1492. Medical historians however date its arrival two centuries earlier.
(Though V.D. was not then the unmentionable it has been till recently, the English generally passed the buck for it to other nationalities, referring to it as *Italian pox, French marbles, Neapolitan scab, Spanish Gout* and *A blow with a French faggot-stick.*)

Precious, Precious coals
16th century oaths, the first a shortening, the second a euphemism for *God's precious body*. Both have rather a Welsh flavour.

Prick
Euphonism for penis. *Prickle,* c. 1550, shortened to read prick.

Rabbit him
18th century corruption of *Drat him* from the earlier *God rot him.*

Rats
Nonsense (U.S.). *The rats* is slang for Delirium Tremens. A strange variant from the 1920s is *The rat's rubbers,* to express surprise.

(No) Robin Hood
Rhyming slang and euphemism for *No bloody good*. First World War.

Rot me, Rot'um
Short for *God rot me* or *them*. 16th to 19th century.

Ruddy
Frequent rhyming euphemism for *Bloody* in Victorian times and later. In 1887 when Gilbert and Sullivan called their new opera RUDDYGORE, with a pun obvious to all, the word outraged Victorian sensibilities. The theatre management did substitute an I for the Y spelling, but could not get Sullivan to agree to change the title further.

Rude, Rood, By the
By the Cross. A medieval oath.

S'
Very common abbreviation of *God's* in 16th to 18th century oaths such as *S'light* and *S'flesh.*

Saints
When Henry VIII decided to ditch the Roman Catholic faith together with most of its saints and martyrs, a fertile source of oaths dried up. Up till then you could suit the saint in your oath to the occasion, calling on *St Crispin* if your shoe pinched (he was patron saint of cobblers), *St Anthony* if you lost something, *St Loy* if you were a blacksmith and the horse kicked you, and so on. There were many droll-sounding oaths on different saintly appendages, such as *By St Paul's thumb, By St Benet's boot, By St Quenet's belly, and* so forth – oaths which have no significance for us today. Now even our national saint has lost status: the oath on his name has dwindled to a mere *By George.* Practically our only surviving saintly oath is the vapid *My sainted aunt.*

Sakes alive, Laws sakes, La Sakes
Mainly U.S. 19th century euphemisms for *Lord's sake. Criminy sakes alive* is *For Christ's sake.*

(By the) Salmon, So help me salmon
Not an angler's oath, but a beggar's curse from Elizabethan times or earlier, *Saloman* was thieves' cant for altar or mass.

(Pon my) Sam
Upon my word. Late Victorian. Various origins have been put forward. It could be (i) the natural development of *Salmon,* the beggar's oath (see above), (ii) a reference to Uncle Sam, the legendary American Meat-Inspector who stamped the initials U.S. on the barrels he passed, or (iii) a reference to General Sir Samuel James Browne V.C., 1824–1901, inventor of the Sam Browne belt worn by officers. (An old Somersetshire woman heard recently using the expression thought she was referring to her military husband's belt.)

Sam Hill, What the
An old-fashioned euphemism for *What the hell.* Was there an eponymous Samuel Hill?

Sblid
North Country dialect form of *God's blood.*

S'blood
See *Blood.*

Sbobs
17th to 19th century corruption of *God's body* or *babe.*

Sbores
17th century oath, rather obscure. It strikes the right note of fashionable ennui for a Restoration beau, but *Bore* in this sense only became established later in the language. Perhaps *Sbores* is a corruption of *God's pores* (the same type of oath as *God's guts, God's bones,* etc.) or an abbreviation of *God's pure ——?*

Sbud
Gallant's minced form of *S'Blood* (*or S'bodikins?*).

Screw you
Euphemism for a four-letter verb but not much of an improvement. A fairly recent addition to the coarse swearer's vocabulary, dating from the late 18th century.

Sdeath
One of Elizabeth I's favourite oaths, and later the subject of a disagreement between Charles II and his Licenser of Plays. The Licenser was worried about passing *Sdeath* and similar expressions for the stage. Charles had no doubts. *Sdeath* and the like were mere 'asseverations', he said, and 'no oaths' at all.

Sdeins, Sdiggers
17th century abbreviations of *God's deynes,* or dignity, and *God's daggers.*

Seduce my ancient footwear
Pedantic euphemism, not as pithy as the original monosyllables.

Shades of Captain Kidd, The departed Greeks, P.T. Barnum (q.v.)
Trivial jokey U.S. oaths, vestiges of the ancient practice of swearing by your own (or someone else's) ancestors, which was not trivial at all. (Among the Maoris, for instance, *Go and cook your grandfather* would be a savage curse*.)

Shankers and Bubos stand off
Rabelaisian oath. Another uninhibited 17th century reference to V.D. (*Shankers* is for *Chancre; Bubos* were the pimples associated with V.D.)

*Ernest Crawley. OATH, CURSE AND BLESSING.

Sheckles
Cockney oath, late 19th century. Probably a euphemism along the same lines as *Shoot* and *Shucks*.

Shit and compounds
Etymologically the same as *Shoot,* a frequent euphemism, and of ancient Indo-European ancestry. In the sense 'to defecate' the verb first appeared in the 14th century. The noun came a century later. Both were certainly more acceptable then than now: in a 16th century play even a clergyman calls a fellow curate a *Shitten lout,* and Ben Jonson writing for the Court had his characters exchanging the odd '*Shit o' your head*'. Swift too occasionally employed the contemptuous dialect forms *Shittletidee* and *Shittencumshites.* After Swift *Shit* more or less disappeared from literature and polite conversation. As a colloquialism it continued, particularly in various graphic compounds such as *Shitsack* (a Nonconformist minister), *Shitehawk* and *Shitepoke* (both birds with unendearing personal habits).
Usage as an expletive started in the 19th century and is now widespread, not only spoken but written (in contemporary pop magazines, for instance). Some of the best modern compounds and catchphrases are from the U.S. and Commonwealth English: the Canadian *Then the shit will really hit the fan* (then there will be disastrous results) and *To stand out like a shithouse in the fog* (i.e. not at all); the Australian *Shit a brick;* the U.S. *Holy shit, Tough shit* and *Shit out of luck* (often shortened to *T.S.* and *S.O.L.*).

Shit, Piss and corruption
Expressive expletive, originally R.A.F. World War II slang for bad weather with rain and flak.

Shittletidee
Nonsense. Rude version (mainly dialect) of *Fiddledidee.*

Shoot, Shucks, Shoot a weasel
Euphemisms for *Shit.*

Sink me, Sink'em
Popular 17th and 18th century oaths, probably originally nautical. In Bunyan's cautionary tale THE LIFE AND DEATH OF MR BADMAN (1690) Mr Badman's second wife can give as good as she gets, 'oath for oath and curse for curse ... damn her and sink her and the like'.

(By) Sire and damn
Restoration oath, all right if you like weak puns.

Skin, By my father's
Early English work-a-day oath. 15th and 16th century.

Sleeping cripe
U.S. euphemism for *Jesus Christ,* rather a long way from the original.

Slice, Slid, Slidikins, Sluck, Slud
17th and 18th century abbreviations and corruptions of *God's life, God's (eye) lid, God's luck, God's blood.*

Smash man Geordie
Durham pitman's oath, recorded from the 19th century.

Smash me/my eyes
North Country oaths.

Smoley hoke
Unnecessary U.S. spoonerism for *Holy smoke.*

Snails
God's nails. 15th to 18th century. Sounds incongruous to modern ears but the horrible pun didn't seem to bother earlier users. Perhaps the weird modern U.S. *Great crawling snails* carries echoes of the older oath.

Snakes, Holy, Suffering. The snake's hips
U.S. petty oaths. Perhaps references to the snakes you're supposed to see in D.T.s?

Sneaks, Sneagues
Corruption of *God's nigs* or *nails.*

Sneck up, Snick up
16th century equivalent of *Go hang yourself.* Literally: put a latch on your mouth.

Snibs
Sucks to you. Probably from the early English *snib,* to reprove or chide.

Snigs, Sniggers
Not *What a giggle* but another of the innumerable 17th and 18th century corruptions of *God's nigs.* (There's also a Victorian descendant *Ill be sniggered.*)

Snollygoster
Corruption of *Holy Ghost,* recorded from Nebraska.

Snooks, Holy
Snooks probably stands for *Spooks* (Saints).

Snowns
Corruption of *God's wounds*. See *Wounds*.

Sod, Sod it, Off
Sod is a long established abbreviation for *Sodomite*. In the 19th century *Sod it* and *Sod off* became common lower class expletives. Thanks to Mrs Sheila Cossey for the following reminiscence of her mother, born in 1888 and brought up in the Cotswolds: 'She used to come out with several spectacular phrases, rolling them out as a single word. When exasperated she would say "*Sod it all Miss Weston till tomorrow*".' (See also *Miss Weston.*)

Son of a bitch
An 18th century insult which has become friendly, though not invariably so, over the years. President Nixon, midst Watergate 1973, gave an example of both the uses when he said 'The Democrats would . . . say that I am a lying *son of a bitch* and the Republicans that I may be lying but that I am their *son of a bitch*'. *Son of a bitch* was also the name of a popular turn of the century stew favoured by Texan cowboys. (A common U.S. euphemism was *Son of a biscuit eater*.)

Son of a gun
Now approving. In the 18th century just the reverse: it meant a soldier's bastard.

Speed the wombats
No prizes for placing this one. In return for the *Gawd*'s, *Blimey*'s and *Bloody*s exported down under in the 19th century, we are now importing a crop of vigorous new Aussie oaths such as this. See also *Starve, Stone, Strewth* and *Strike.*

Spit o' my hand, Spit my death
Victorian Cockney oaths.

Split my windpipe
According to a late 17th century dictionary, 'a silly curse in use among the Beaux'.

Splunter and oons, Splice my old shoes, Smite my timbers
A string of nautical oaths from Tobias Smollett, the 18th century novelist, goalbird (for libel) and surgeon's mate on a British man-o'-war.

Stap my vitals, My breath
Restoration oaths. *Stap* is the 18th century spelling for *Stop*.

(My) Stars and Garters
19th century lower class oath: the coachman in Dickens' NICHOLAS NICKLEBY uses it. The *Star and Garter* is a popular pub name, referring of course to the ancient Order of Knights of the Garter. The Victorian oath probably refers to a particular pub, the Star and Garter on Richmond Hill which was slightly notorious at that period. It was a rather pretentious building which caused a bankruptcy in 1810, and in the latter half of the century became a fashionable port of call for a drive out of London. It was noted for its exorbitant prices.

Starve the lizards, The birdies
Vivid Australian incredulity.

Steups
West Indian sucking of teeth to express contempt.

(God) Stiffen it, Stiffen the crows, Snakes
God stiffen was low Victorian slang meaning *God destroy it.* (The semantics are the same in 'stiff' or corpse.) Probably the Victorian oath is the origin of the modern Australian *Stiffen the Crows,* etc.

Stone me, The crows, The mopokes
More Australian amazement. C.f. *Stiffen* and *Starve*. The *Mopokes* are owls.

Streuth, Strewth Bruce
Strine telescoping of *God's truth* plus the inevitable Christian name (c.f. *Gawd Aggie, Blimey Charlie,* etc.). Recommended Australian pronunciation is a long drawn-out drawl.

Strike me and combinations
Short for *God strike me.* Originally a stylish oath. Restoration beaux, like Vanburgh's Lord Foppington, would exclaim *Strike me speechless.* Later the oath lost caste and Cockneys and Australians made it their own, by tagging on adjectives such as *Blind, Dumb, Lucky, Pink, Perp, Up a gum tree* (q.v.).

Strike me up a blue gum
Famous Australian oath. The eucalyptus or blue gum tree has a smooth trunk which makes it hard to climb up.

Suffering catfish, Sassafrass, Sea serpents, Snakes (q.v.), Whangdoodles
U.S. trivial oaths in which *Suffering* is a substitute for *Saint(ed)*.

Sugar
Not as innocent as it first appears. Combine *Shit* and *Bugger* and what do you get?

Swelp me Bob, Davy, My greens, Taters, Ten men
Cockney barrowboys, variations on the original *So help me God.* See also *Bob* and *Greens.*

Swiggered, I'll be, also Digswiggered, Bumswiggered, Jimswiggled
Early 20th century facetious oaths from the U.S. Probably meaningless, but perhaps with memories of *Bugger* and the old English *Swig,* to drink deeply (and get drunk). Similar to *Bumswizzled* (q.v.).

Swill
Workaday 17th century oath, abbreviation of *God's will.*

Swiss cheese, Holy sweet cheesecakes
U.S. euphemisms for *Jesus Christ* making good use of assonance. C.f. *Cheese and crust, Caesar's crutch.*

Swob, Swop me Bob, Dickey
Variants of *Swelp me Bob,* etc.

Sworbote
Medieval oath, a corruption of *God's forbote,* God's prohibition.

Swounds
Abbreviation of *God's wounds,* a form popular in Elizabethan and Restoration times. See *Wounds.*

Tare an' ouns
Irish oath of the huntin' shootin' fishin' crowd. Corruption of (*Christ's*) *tears and wounds.*

Tarn, Tarnal, Tarnation
Mainly U.S., dating from the War of Independence, by telescoping

Eternal damnation. The refrain of a 'Rebel' song of 1775 runs: 'We didn't care one *Tarnal* bit.'

Taxidermist, Go and see a
Polite pedantry for *Get stuffed.*

Therewith
Not much of a swear word maybe, but used as one by genteel Victorians who fancied their German. (German *Damit,* therewith.)

Thunder and – combinations
Thunder and turf, Thunder, furies and damnation, Oons and Thunder were fashionable imprecations in the 18th and 19th centuries. Later U.S. examples, such as *Thunder and scissors, Thunder and gimpson root* (q.v.), and *Thunder and blue lightning* were probably inspired by the oaths of German immigrants, *Donner und Blitzen,* etc.

Timbers, Shiver my, Dash my
Traditional oaths for old salts. On board ship the *Timbers* were the stout pieces of wood which curved upwards from the keel – unlikely to be *Shivered* or *Dashed* and dangerous if they were.

Toast yer blimin eyebrows
Victorian lower class slang with *Go to hell and* ... understood.

Tomago, Go to
Australian euphemism for *Go to hell. Tomago,* pronounced 'Tommy-go', is a town in S.E. Australia. The expression probably grew out of *Hell and Tommy* (q.v.).

Tonnay
West Indian oath, corruption of *Tonnerre.*

Turd
Good old English crudity. If you wanted to hurl a basic Elizabethan insult at a fellow yokel, you could try *A turd i' your teeth, A turd for you,* or *Goodman turd.*

Turds and candlesticks
Notable only as the favourite expletive of one John Gabriel Stedman, 18th century soldier and adventurer. (Thanks to Mrs I. W. Richardson.)

Twat (you)
Equivalent to *Cunt* but less well-known. Rarely seen in print. When Browning used it in the last lines of PIPPA PASSES he dropped one of the biggest literary clangers ever:

'Then owls and bats,
Cowls and twats,
Monks and nuns, in a cloister's moods
Adjourn'.

Ud, Uds
16th and 17th century corruptions of *God's,* as in the examples below.

Udsbud
Corruption of *God's blood.*

Uds niggers noggers
God's nails (from the older English *nigs,* nails).

Uds wountlinkins
God's (little) wounds. Popular oath of the 18th century tavern trade, according to Ned Ward, publican of the King's Head Tavern, Chancery Lane. (See Introduction pp. 31–2).

U.B.Dd.
Euphemistic initials. For others see *B.F.*

(Miss) Weston
In combinations such as *My oath, Miss Weston, Sod it all, Miss Weston,* is an apology for strong language. The reference is to Dame Agnes Weston (died 1918), founder and organiser of the 'Sailors' Rest' hostels, a keen worker for naval temperance and a stickler for propriety.

Whoreson
Much used Elizabethan and Jacobean pejorative adjective. Probably equivalent in value to *Bloody* today.

William the Third
Rhyming euphemism for *Turd.*

Wounds
Abbreviation of *God's wounds.* Originally the oath was a very serious one, and a profanity of the first rank. The Five Wounds of Christ (in His hands, feet and side) were a common theme in medieval

religious art and literature. Swift said the oath was first used by Sir John Perrot, allegedly one of Henry VIII's illegitimate sons, but it was probably much earlier. It was certainly durable: according to Swift again it was still a stock oath in his day.

Wriggling tripe
Farfetched U.S. euphemism for *Jesus Christ* via *Cripe*.

Yfacs, Yfegs
See *Fac*.

Z
Abbreviation of *God's* in many 16th to 19th century oaths such as *Zdeath, Zbud, Zfoot, Zlead,* (*God's lid*).

Zookers
Corruption of *God's hooks* or *nails*.

Zoons, Zounds, Zounters, Zauns
All variants of (*God's*) *wounds* (q.v.). Pronunciation as well as spelling seems to have varied. According to Rigadoon, the affected gallant in Farquhar's LOVE IN A BOTTLE of 1698, '*Zoons* is only us'd by the disbanded Officers and Bullies: but *Zauns* is the Beaux pronunciation'.

Zooterkins
Said to have been a favourite oath with Elizabeth's court ladies, probably a corruption of *Zouters* or *Zookers* (q.v.).